MAC & IRENE
A WWII SAGA

MARGOT McMAHON

AQUARIUS PRESS

Detroit, Michigan

Mac & Irene: A WWII Saga
© 2021 by Margot McMahon

ISBN 978-1-7379876-0-4
Library of Congress Control Number: 2021947584

Margot McMahon Collection

Disclaimer: This book is based, in part, upon actual events and persons. However, some characters and incidents portrayed herein are fictitious. Any similarity to any actual person, living or dead, or to any actual event is entirely coincidental and unintentional.

Cover art: (c) Franklin McMahon Estate

AQUARIUS PRESS, www.AquariusPress.net

Printed in the United States of America

Contents

INTRODUCTION

To engage with one of Franklin McMahon's drawings is to be swept into a moment. It is quite apart from looking at a photograph. In the latter, one is being taught: the photo is truth, or so it claims, and you are charged with finding a way within yourself to accept that truth. What argument could be raised to compete with this technological testimony? The photo makes no attempt to persuade or influence. It speaks with authority, and you must reconcile yourself to it or tilt at your antiquated windmills.

"Mac's" drawings are different. They beckon, they welcome you in. There is beauty in the color—or in its absence. The fluidity of his strokes offer a degree of comfort. The drawing shows a world that you may enter, be part of, and having entered, your own reference, your own sensibility and reality is also welcome. Mac provides his own sense of the moment, but the rest is up to you. Because you are comfortable, because you are a part of this world, you are open to its inherent truth.

A drawing of a beloved Chicago setting puts you in warm, welcoming Chicago; you have no doubt that this is its character. Who is with you? That is up to you. You are free to supplement Mac's vision with your own. Mac doesn't coerce you to accept his version of things—he convinces you.

Where does this trustworthiness come from? Margot McMahon, in the pages to come, reveals it. You join her as she approaches the home, all full of sensory memory. The familiar is flooding her in the aftermath of her mother's passing and her father's fading. There is a certain danger here; will she be overwhelmed by the weight of memory and infirmity? She, and we, approach the threshold with timidity, but with the courage that her love and sense of duty confer.

And so a life begins to unfold, seemingly dim from time and weathering. The sentences are halting and provide only a hint of detail. They carry us along, confusingly at first. We gain a sense of where we are, then of when we are, then of what is happening, then of what is being felt. Here and there a drawing appears on the page, or a photo of a piece of life's detritus.

This collage of words, feelings, illustrations, and ephemera are coalescing into their own book-drawing (or, given Margot's authorship, perhaps it is a book-sculpture), and once again, we are welcomed in. It's a lovely ride.

Mac's journey from innocent youngster, finding a seemingly preordained love and an emerging artistic gift, to awestruck, dazed soldier-navigator, to the few moments of terror and existential amazement where life and future lay in the balance, and then finally to an unreality wherein life is suspended and hell is breaking through civilization's veneer, is told with an eerie distance. We are inside Mac's soul, but to him and to us, it all seems to be happening to someone else. He is observing his life taking place from afar, even as he experiences it and shares it with us. It is thus utterly unsurprising that he transfers it to paper, or to whatever medium avails at any given moment. This is the artist's consciousness. So when we see the illustrations from time to time as we go through these pages, we are viewing the familiar. Here, the Mac we are permitted access to does not so much live his life as he records it. It is not that he lives an inauthentic life; rather, he has a uniquely examined life—because of his artistic gift. That part of him, an indispensable part, is the part shared in these pages.

Therein lies the authenticity that breeds the trust that we feel in Mac. The life of the artist, and the life in his art, are indistinguishable. Savor it, as it unfolds in these pages. Then, like me, you will luxuriate in his work, and own an enduring gratitude for the work and the life.

—Andrew C. Lipka
Princeton Junction, NJ
February 2021

PRELUDE

In his eighties, Dad handed me books like *Monuments Men, The Wooden Horse* and *The Great Escape* to tell me his story. We talked and I wrote, as his energy waned, while his wit recalled minute details. My questions got cryptic answers such as, "It was kind of like that." I filled in the ambiguous lines of glazed-over stories and compiled answers. Moments evolved into his story of interwoven truths, both mentioned and imagined, until one became the other. With each TIA and stroke, childhood memories surfaced of his old friends, or dates with Mom. I have come to recognize the connection of human affection that explains that we are here and still wondering. That we are going to die means we are the lucky ones.

~

Dad's stone home, with a circular drive, was nestled in an oak clearing. The roar of the nearby highway triggered memories of the waves on Lake Michigan with a chronic rhythm that rose up the far side of the highway berm, arched, then dropped in a wall of sound. Walking through the constant din, I chafed in jeans and a sweatshirt, too warm for the peaking 68 degrees. The asphalt driveway under my sneakers steamed as I stepped through the highway hum.

Droning highway monotony was behind me as the thrush and red-winged black bird calls came into focus. My heartbeat matched that of the resonating crickets. I was calmed with the rhythms of the woods. A rustling of oak leaves caught the breeze, then the familiar clatter of cattails, until a dense tranquility of nature filled my heart. I was soothed with the cicadas' cadences rising and falling. The brightness of the sun gave way to the shadow of the woods. The chirping, squawking, trilling of birds and clacking, rustling and creaking of branches stilled the chaos of my loss, reordering my life after burying my mom several months before. The momentary communion with nature entered my soul as a consoling friend. I was further pacified as I passed between aromatic weeping cherry and fragrant crab apple trees before entering the side door of Dad's mid-century modern home. The scent reminded me of Mom's making of crab apple jelly with my kids as I turned the nickel nob and pushed open the wooden door. Silence resounded through the long hallway. No familiar footsteps of Mom greeted me at the door. A chair squeaked in Dad's studio.

"Good day." I broke the silence.

"Well, there you are. I'm glad you came," he said. "I'll just finish up here and be in." Damar varnish, turpentine and beeswax aromas whirled in the hallway. *Smells like home.* I stepped into his studio to see my dad with three paint brushes in his mouth—and palette knives in either hand—before a vertical painting of a thistle in an ochre glow. A thistle patch grew outside his window. I knew not to interrupt; I had to wait for a lunchtime conversation.

"Looks good," I said. "I'll put lunch in the fridge and be in the living room, no hurry." I walked past my mother's empty office and down the narrow hall to the kitchen. A deer gazed at me, or at its reflection, in the wide windows. I gazed back. This was the same sun-dappled, wooded yard in which Daniel and I met playing croquet several years before we celebrated our marriage. We jumped into that pool on our first date after a sweltering Westside day. The deer twitched its tail and dashed into the buckthorn. This was the yard Dad and I raked, mowed and shoveled. We were building a new type of reliance with one another there.

I tossed out the prior week's uneaten food from the fridge and replaced it with fresh meals on the top shelf. In the living room, I sunk into the family's couch. My fatigue was a side-effect of bending time. Mom had been a master time-bender, raising nine children as an award-winning travel writer. Had it only been a year since my father, mother and I sat in that very room with my infant daughter? I had thought Mom was starting to age then. Nothing could have prepared me for her sudden death. *The more important it is, the less is told.* I had missed my mother's first stroke because no one told me at college. There was the unmentioned pneumonia but no forewarning that my mom had months to live. Until the night of her death, who knew she had a lung disease? I scanned my memory for clues. None.

"Will you come to the back room for a minute?" Dad asked. "I want to show you a few things." We stepped down into the den, then up two steps single file, down two more steps into the narrow hallway lit by high, horizontal windows in the late morning sun. Turpentine and Damar varnish vapors faintly traveled with us down the hall.

"How is the painting going?" I asked. We passed my bedroom,

with my sculptures on the low shelf that ran the length of the room. My family stayed there often.

"It is winning," he said. We entered his bedroom, which my sisters and I had prepared for our mother's return with an oxygen pump and a wheelchair. I hadn't been in the room since. My mother never left the hospital. My father opened his top drawer and opened a small box.

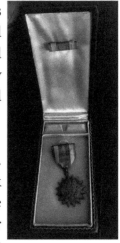

"These are my Army Air Force medals."

"You have Army medals?" I asked in surprise.

As if giving a tour, Dad walked over to a desk peninsula and pulled out a fireproof box. "These are important financial documents your mother kept." *What an unprecedented moment. Dad is sharing secrets I have never been privy to. He's a decorated WWII vet? Why?* I couldn't imagine him with an Air Force medal pinned on his pocket. Was there a ceremony? Dad told me he'd wash up and meet me at the dining room table.

I warmed up soup and tossed a salad, mixed powdered iced tea and squeezed lemon on everything, barely noticing what I was doing. I prepped our meal on autopilot while I struggled to overcome my loss and the task ahead. I had thank-you notes for the memorial service to finish and was behind on a sculpture due by Christmas. I set two plates at the end of the long table, with a dozen empty chairs, and sat facing the kitchen. My mother's vacant chair faced out toward the walls of windows and the oak grove. Even though she was a writer, I would never fully know her library of stories and experiences, but I assumed I'd be able to ask Dad. After sliding aside his nearly full bowl and plate and my empty dishes, I caught my breath and slowly exhaled,

"When did you and Mom fall in love?"

"Not sure about your mother," he replied, uncertain. "It might have been my birthday at the ice cream parlor, when I fell in love with her." Without looking away, I grabbed the phone message notebook and scribbled furiously to catch his phrases. "The gang met at the Esquire for ice cream after school. I had just locked up my job at *Extensions Magazine* as a cartoonist and was feeling pretty good

about things. Irene and Charlotte stopped in from the Madison Avenue bus. They were coming home from their first year at Teacher's College." I lost my sense of time in his story as Dad recreated the moment as if it happened yesterday.

~

September, 1938 Murmurations, Oak Park, Illinois

"I'd really like to fly in one of those!" Mac mentioned to his friend Jack at the Esquire ice cream shop. He pointed up as a plane roared overhead.

I imagined this as an Archie and Veronica comic strip with the gang gathering after school. Irene was behind Mac, ordering her regular hot fudge sundae with peanuts. The pastel pink-and-blue booths were mostly filled with Trinity and Fenwick students. Mac ate a macaroon cookie as he sat with his cousin and a few friends around a circular table on his and Jack Duggan's birthday.

"Oh, so would I!" Irene said loudly. Jack and Mac looked over. "Traveling, seeing new cities, living elsewhere is my dream," she added. "I can live anywhere once I get my teacher's license," she said within a balloon of text above her flip hairstyle.

"I would like to fly to D.C. and New York, with you." Mac surprised himself with his awkward boldness. *It is my birthday celebration after all,* he thought. "We could land on Lake George and traverse the Adirondacks." Mac tried to dig out of his blush.

Irene had no idea where the Adirondacks were, yet gave a knowing smile. Landing anywhere else sounded good to her.

"Sky's the limit," she agreed. "I'd like to see St. Louis and Atlanta, Miami and Santa Fe. Let's start with those!"

"How about around the world?" Mac asked. I imagined the cartoon strip had a scene of the two of them waving from an open-air prop plane with a globe below them.

"Why…(not!)" Another propeller plane flew over, drowning out the "not."

"That one is headed to Denver," Irene said. And so began their guessing-the-destination as planes propelled through the skies. The friends melted away in my comic strip frame.

~

"When do you think Mom fell in love with you?" I asked. I refilled our glasses of lemonade. Dad looked at the surface in the glass, watched the ripples settle.

"I may have started to have a chance with your mother during a Porgy and Bess song at a Sienna Dance," Dad said. I remembered Mom melting over Gershwin's orchestration at the Fourth of July celebration behind Deerpath School. Mom loved the Fourth of July. Dad didn't.

"Mom liked Gershwin's *Porgy and Bess* at the Fourth of July concerts," I said.

My thoughts wandered to the parish gym where my parents had met, where maybe Mom had fallen in love with Dad. My father was a senior in high school. My mother had already started Teacher's College with her friends Charlotte and Madeline.

Besides the French Club, dance committee, football and boxing teams, Dad was the cartoonist of Fenwick's yearbook. Mac was thrilled with the heady mix of anonymity and authority over his own sense of self and welcomed the validation to become himself. He sold stocks to family and friends for stamp money to mail out his cartoons. If the cartoon was published, he shared the profit with his contributors, beginning the delicate balance of his creative spirit and commerce. He trained, nurtured, then offered his talent freely. The practice took a certain asceticism and carefree abandon. The giving created the void to conjure more art while building a connection to community through art. "It helps if you have success when you are young," he told us.

~

1939 Sienna Dance

Twisted crepe paper streamers and balloons were taped from the basketball net to the walls. A teen chatted with two friends, a boy and girl. Another girl walked in their direction. Her hair was either tied in a ponytail with a ribbon or held in a flip with hairspray. One girl was Mom, like in her high school photographs. She glanced at a boy who looked like my brother.

Irene couldn't break away from the conversation she was in with a dark-haired boy and his cockamamie idea to enlist in the Army.

"Len, why not divert your civic drive to helping poor children who go to school hungry?" Irene said after she finished an explanation of what Dorothy Day might have said against anything but pacifist action. "Let's feed students before school."

"I'd rather be a lieutenant than a jail bird," Len replied. All of them, Irene and Mac and their friends, had met in 1938 at St. Catherine's Sienna Dance. The gaggle of America's first teenagers included Irene Leahy, Charlotte Monday and Madeline Duggan, who loved to shop at Carson's or Field's between transferring buses from Francis Parker's Teacher's College to home.

"Have you ever seen navy polka-dotted scarves?" Irene asked Madeline.

"I love the shoes. So many heels to choose from," Madeline said.

"Why would you enlist, Len? It's not America's problem." Charlotte begged for a reason.

"What's bigger than a world war…?" Len asked, in his riddling way, to divert the question.

"Lo and behold! If it isn't a long drink-of-water!" Irene smiled at Mac as he walked up to the group. A magazine was rolled in his back pocket. Clarence MacDonald, the red-haired Fenwick class math-mind, joined them and listened. Len asked "quiet" Clarence about his summer job in the University of Chicago physics lab. Clarence shrugged.

"Hi, Mac," Madeline and Charlotte said at the same time.

"Hey, Mac, what's bigger than a world war and smaller than a thumb?" Len asked again.

"The bullet you dodge," Mac replied, a bit peeved to be conversing about Europe's war.

"That's it, Mac!" Len said. "Better than the one I had... I was going to say the bullet that gets you." He laughed. Several of the teens chuckled. Mac opened the *Colliers* magazine and showed Irene his published cartoon. They all leaned in to look. Emotions muddled in their huddle—pride from a friend, jealousy from one, a glow from Irene and dismay from another. Mac was learning to deal with reactions to his art.

Billie Holiday's rendition of "Summertim*e*" from *Porgy and Bess* began.

"Irene, would you like to dance?"

Mac took Irene's gloved hand into his and they disappeared onto the dance floor. Her hand, lightly and gracefully, welcomed his. His hand, gently and shyly, supported hers.

"*Happiness is the natural flower of duty.*"

"You're right about chipping in, Len." Clarence finally spoke as other teens came over to chat. "If America doesn't chip in, we might be the only ones left, with no one around to help us. I've seen papers around the office about awful ideas being tried out in Germany." The group turned sullen with dreary, shocked anger over

Clarence upsetting the dance. One after another, the teens drifted away as Clarence told Len about what he had learned while working in the Manhattan Project lab.

No one knew the horrors of what was emerging in 1938 eastern Germany.

"A lab in Posen is experimenting with chemicals to eradicate starving *volkstum*, ethnic peoples, with gas. Trainloads of people are being transported to the lab but the scientists can't possibly feed them all. They're forcing Jewish people to wear arm bands with yellow stars for ID when transported from Posen to Russia. Their homes are then given to Germans who move in."

"Why isn't this in the papers?" Len asked with an ashen face.

"There is no evidence," Clarence said. Both looked onto the dance floor, a bit dazed.

Nearby, Irene and Mac were humbled in their love. They stared deeply into each other's eyes. They turned and dipped to their living that was easy, oblivious to their summertime surroundings. "Your daddy's rich and your mamma's good-looking..." The music played on. "...So hush little baby, don't you cry..."

Mac twirled Irene, who lightly spun on her right toe. The world was just the two of them. She was caught by her waist in his arm, his right drawing arm, as the song continued to play. Their graduations from high school melted away, the giddy expectations of what they'd do next evaporated into a misty future. This moment was their entire life.

The music faded to an announcer who called the last dance, "... and it will be a slooow one."

"Good night, Irene... Good night Irene," Louie Armstrong's rendition played the last tune of Sienna Night as Mac and Irene walked arm-in-arm to the Washington Street trolley. "Good night Irene, good night, Irene... I'll see you in my dreams..." As the song faded, Mac escorted Irene to Central Park Boulevard in Austin, careful to walk on the street side in case a car splashed puddles.

"Denver!" "L.A.!" they called simultaneously as a propeller plane buzzed above the trees under the moon.

~

When my sixth-grade son Mahon and his friend Ian took an interest in WWII, I arranged with Dad to tell them his story. During a half-day off from school, he sat at his dining room table with the two boys and told them about navigating a B-17 flying fortress over Germany with amazing detail. *Why hadn't I been told his story?* I sat at the far end of our long table for twelve with a video camera running. *Why hadn't I asked?*

"World War II went on for quite a while before the U.S. got into it... not until after Pearl Harbor was attacked. The war went on for a while longer before I got into it," he said. *I can't imagine his sweetheart Irene, the peace lover, or Gramma Mac supporting her only son going to war.* In my mother's boxes, I found a 1942 receipt for a gag Dad sold to *The New Yorker*, so his dream of being a cartoonist for that magazine had already been accomplished. Dad may have looked up from his drawing table and realized he was the last young man in Chicago. Maybe enlisting gave him more control over his future than the newly imposed draft. The mighty maelstrom of destructive energy finally pulled in this only child, this boy with a peace-loving girlfriend. At night, I transcribed his videotaped story, typing it for the skeletal structure of his story. To round out Dad's story, I researched details and cross-checked with him.

~

"So, what have you been writing?" Dad asked. I was relieved he wanted to hear more about his war story, as I was too nervous to mention it.

"I thought you'd never ask." I handed him my notebook. "This might be redundant, but I found supporting facts." Dad's memory flashed, which in turn energized me. I was writing his story—that soothed him with purpose. As the story came to life, Dad unwound. We fulfilled for each other a necessary understanding of what happened. I swelled with finding his past so profoundly, while he relaxed into letting go of having to remember to forget. My dad gently took and read aloud his story of those missions he flew so many years ago.

PARACHUTING ARTIST

Mac spiraled into his hero's journey with the Navy June 19, 1942 with a kiss-charmed photo of Irene in his pocket, his constant mother's encouragement and a rare paternal handshake. He'd deposited a check from *The New Yorker* and enlisted.

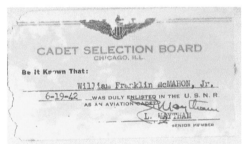

... issue, sent us this snapshot of himsel ....
fellow, who, he says, "made a nasty crack about *our* magazine!"
. . . FRANKLIN McMAHON, our favorite cartoonist (see
page 12), is now in the Navy Air Corps. . . . Your curiosity
concerning our gay cover will be satisfied if you'll ...

"I'd like to learn to fly airplanes," Mac had told his cousin Bob O'Brien, a recruiter, who suggested he join the Navy. *Extensions* magazine kept him on as a stringer, a war correspondent.

"You are mostly on the Earth's surface in the Navy," Bob told him. "The fall is a splash." Mac tested into the Navy Air Force with a spatial intelligence.

~

At Iowa State University, Mac wandered around the Ionic columns and limestone architecture, past ponds with white geese. Math skills were drilled into him day and night in stone-trimmed red brick buildings with PHYSICS carved into limestone plinths. The creamy stone clocktower

First group of air cadets supplied by Chicago's "Fly for Navy" recruiting drive about to learn for the preflight school at the University of Iowa. They're at naval aviation cadet selection board in Board of Trade building.

rang above Iowa's tree-studded hills. The ultra-condensed college training was excruciating, but Mac eeked out cartoons, sometimes photographs, and mailed them to *Extensions*. Mac wrote journal-like telegrams to his mother and Irene. Boxing and push-ups morphed into his cartoons. He practiced collegiate military math in plaster-walled dorms with roommates.

Mac was elated to be flying in giant churning clouds with his eyes in the nose of a plane. He continued his training at Glenview Airbase

while Irene became a United Airlines stewardess. At Glenview Naval Air Station, Mac received orders to sing for Christmastime Navy publicity.

"They were lucky I wasn't *singing*," he joked in blue uniform dress on his way to a mess hall of meat, potatoes, veggies and milk. Mac was on top of the world. He had just flown solo his first time! He took off, flew and landed on January 1st, 1943. It was a rocky landing.

Mac ate meals with his roommates, Nate Kiddawl, Bill Miller, and Joe Hanja. They shaved their stubble after a hot shower with fresh razors and a cold splash of water. Mac considered those "soft days" from his "college experience." They'd race down the stairs and through wooden doors with leaded glass into the cafeteria.

"The plane was flying me," Mac told his friends at dinner. "It might have something to do with I've never driven a car? Don't know how to swim either."

"Why did you enlist in the Navy?" Nate asked.

"It was recommended, but I was misinformed," Mac said with regret. "The plane landed me too high."

Mac washed out of Navy training. A deep-seated loneliness settled in back in Chicago, an uneasiness that the war might end before he'd get to serve. Irene was flying with United from Chicago's airport hub. His buddies moved on to officer training. Mac had been a part of something really big, bigger than all imagining, and he was sidelined.

Months later, Mac enlisted in the Army Air Corps on June 1, 1943 and was assigned to Latrobe, Pennsylvania. He was later promoted to Second Lieutenant and stationed near the industrial plumes of Pittsburgh. Transformed into a Bearcat officer in Army khakis, Mac entered the red brick castle steeples of St. Vincent College for Aviation Cadet Training. Stationed on the rolling hills, Mac spent a month or two in dull, uninspiring mathematics classes.

"As if Math was going to get me out of there," he joked with his mother and Irene during their visit. They sat at Formica-covered cafeteria tables with coffee and chocolate cake for an afternoon visit. Irene and Bess had driven from Chicago to celebrate her teaching degree. Briefly, they'd forgotten a war going on amidst October's glow of changing leaves. Irene planned to be an art teacher. Mac was promoted Commander of a student group.

"They found out I was pretty good at navigation," Mac said. Being an officer who hadn't been promoted through the ranks gave him benefits, and later, detriments. Resentment settled in. The new guy got special treatment, not always friendly. That was how it was.

Mac said goodbye to his mother, then Irene. It was all numbers and geometry, drill and exam, until Mac's visualization of the sky became scientific and mathematical. If the plane's navigation went down, he was trained to guide his plane back to base by studying the constellations.

~

Keeping warm was the hardest thing. Coal was severely rationed.

Every week, a bin was filled and everyone rushed in to fill whatever containers they had for their week's supply. Nate and Mac "scuttlebutted" over C-rations of dehydrated eggs, potatoes and detestable spam. Oatmeal broke the monotony.

"Ahhh, so cold!" Mac's fingers were blue even though he puffed warm air into his gloves. The ink in the pen seemed to freeze before a letter was finished. The damp coal would not light; he could not get his stove damper working.

Mac knocked on Joe's door. Joe's room was warmer to finish his letters. The next night, Joe came to Mac's room to write letters and commiserate. They stayed warm with half the coal. It was cold everywhere except by the fire in the mess hall and in their electric flight suits. They were relieved to be called to fly, where they could get warm in electric suits and boots plugged into the rising plane.

~

In July 1944, Mac was transferred by train to warmer Randolph Field in Texas with the other Second Lieutenants. Mac was absorbed in another game of Hearts on the monotonous trip when a guy slipped on a banana peel; the busload erupted in guffaws. Another napping guy's hands were put in warm water which made him urinate to laughter. Even the staunchest Second Lieutenant smiled a bit. Train after train passed by, filled with whooping Army troops waving hats. Mac was humbled to play a part in the enormousness of the nation's war effort.

"There is something about the Nazis and the Jews, but I'm not sure what?" Mac wrote to his mother. By 1942, the "Big Three", Churchill of Britain, Roosevelt of the United States and Stalin of the Soviet Union, controlled Allied Policy. The U.S. entered the war in December, 1941 after Pearl Harbor was attacked.

"The U.S. flies in daylight," Mac wrote. "Americans go for bombing strategic sites like ball bearing factories, train tracks or stations." He used his best handwriting. "The British Commonwealth, including Canada, Australia, New Zealand, Newfoundland and South Africa, are gaining in air superiority over the Germans." Sweat dripped on the page as he was so hot. The desert reflected the steaming sun. "The British Royal Airforce flies at night and drops flare bombs into the center of German cities." His hand cramped a bit. "Germans occupy bases in Guernsey and Jersey to blitz London for fifty-seven consecutive nights, wiping out 40,000 civilians. They bombed another dozen or so British cities. Churchill retaliated by bombing Berlin and radio broadcasting his speech the 'Battle of Britain'. We arrived after the largest sustained aerial bombing to date." Mac checked his spelling, rewrote the note on better paper in his best cursive, and addressed an air mail envelope while the ink dried. He bought a three-cent stamp, mailed the envelope and collapsed in bed.

INSTRUCTIONS TO APPLICANTS

FOR APPOINTMENT AS AVIATION CADET (AIR CREW)

ELIGIBILITY: Army Aviation Cadet Training (Air Crew) is open to all men, between the ages of 17 to 26 (inclusive) married or single, who have been a Citizen of the United States for a period of at least ten (10) years and are found mentally, morally and physically qualified.

1. The following papers must be furnished the Aviation Cadet Board, before the Mental Examination can be taken:

    a. One application blank, completely filled out and signed.

    b. Certified copy of your Birth or Baptismal Certificate, or other satisfactory proof of birth.

    c. Three letters of recommendation from reputable non-related citizens.

    d. 17 year old applicants must have parents consent blanks signed by at least one parent and notarized.

    e. 18 to 26 year old applicants must have a letter from their local Selective Service boards, stating that applicant has not been ordered for induction and that he is not employed in any occupation essential to the War effort.

2. Application and allied papers being in order you will be given the Aviation Cadet Mental Examination at such time and place specified by the Cadet Board.

3. If you are found qualified, mentally, you will be required to proceed, at your own expense, to a station, specified by the board, which is equipped to accomplish final type physical examination for flying duty. You will be furnished a letter of authorization to present to the Flight Surgeon.

4. After you have completed your physical and mental examination, you will return to your home and await the results of your examination and furher instructions.

5. If you are under 18 years of age and found Mentally, Morally and Physically qualified, you will be enlisted in the Army Air Corps Enlisted Reserve. You will be required to designate a month in which you desire a call to ⸝duty, this month must be after you have reached your 18th birthday and befo. ⸝ave reached the age of 18 years and 6 months.

6. If you are between 18 and 26 years of age (inclusive) and found Mentally, Morally and Physically qualified, you will be furnished a letter of qualification and instructed to report to your Local Selective Service Board for Voluntary Induction. This must be completed before a period of 90 days have elapsed. If you are ordered to report for induction by your Local Selective Board before you volunteer, your status as a qualified applicant is automatically terminated. After voluntary induction has been completed you will be placed on an inactive status and called to active duty after a lapse of 7 days.

The note Bess McMahon received was severely edited:

"There is something about the ███████████ but I'm not sure what's going on? The U.S. ███████████████████████ ██ The British Commonwealth, including Canada, Australia, New Zealand, Newfoundland and South Africa, ███████████ the Germans." The British Royal Airforce flies at night and drops ██ ██ so, British cities. Churchill retaliated by bombing Berlin and radio broadcasting his speech the "*Battle of Britain*". We arrived after the largest sustained aerial bombing to date.

Much Love, Your Son Mac

Bess McMahon (mother), Mac and Irene Leahy

Mac and Irene

15 November 1944

Mother dear-

I am sitting in Jack's room writing this – his is warm and mine is cold. Couldn't get my fire going tonight. He couldn't get his going last night and came into my room to write. These stoves have no grate and they're hard to operate as there is no draft up through them. I will have to see if I can make myself a grate of some kind.

This is our hardest problem – keeping warm. Coal is severely rationed and very hard to get. They issue us some every week – put it in the bin and everybody rushes to fill up every available container. Perhaps it is better if we share our fires in this manner – Jack making them one night, I another. It is quite cold everywhere we go during the day too. The class rooms and mess hall is not very warm unless you get a seat by the fire. The chow is very good

though and they usually have
warm soup so it isn't so bad.
Probably the warmest place will
be the airplane as we have electric
suits — I'm hoping it will be
warm anyhow.

The class work is not hard —
mostly review.

Hope things are going well
with you as far as business and
the new abode are concerned. I am
anxiously awaiting word from you
Perhaps I will get a letter soon.

Did I tell you the N'Yorker
got there all right — at P.O.E., so
I guess you can continue sending
them or have them send me the
overseas edition for the next 6 months
or so. I enjoy the ads though and
they are not in the overseas edition.
I will send you copies of the more
interesting issues of "Stars + Stripes"

My love for now
Mac

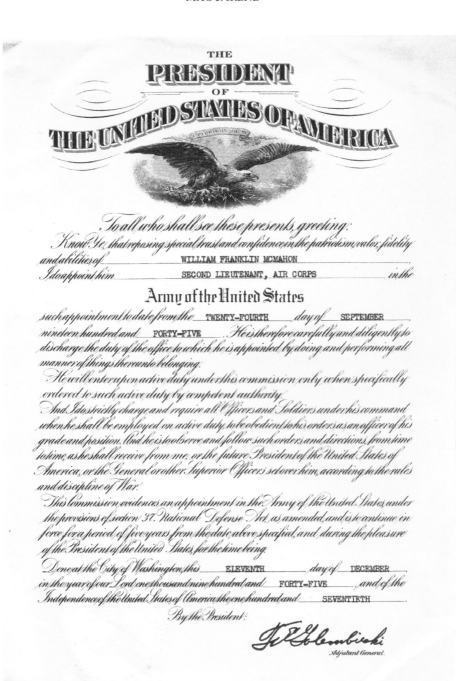

THE

PRESIDENT

OF

THE UNITED STATES OF AMERICA

To all who shall see these presents, greeting:

Know Ye, that reposing special trust and confidence in the patriotism, valor, fidelity and abilities of WILLIAM FRANKLIN MCMAHON

I do appoint him SECOND LIEUTENANT, AIR CORPS *in the*

Army of the United States

such appointment to date from the TWENTY-FOURTH *day of* SEPTEMBER *nineteen hundred and* FORTY-FIVE *. He is therefore carefully and diligently to discharge the duty of the office to which he is appointed by doing and performing all manner of things thereunto belonging.*

He will enter upon active duty under this commission only when specifically ordered to such active duty by competent authority.

And I do strictly charge and require all Officers and Soldiers under his command when he shall be employed on active duty to be obedient to his orders as an officer of his grade and position. And he is to observe and follow such orders and directions, from time to time, as he shall receive from me, or the future President of the United States of America, or the General or other Superior Officers set over him, according to the rules and discipline of War.

This commission evidences an appointment in the Army of the United States, under the provisions of section 37, National Defense Act, as amended, and is to continue in force for a period of five years from the date above specified, and during the pleasure of the President of the United States, for the time being.

Done at the City of Washington, this ELEVENTH *day of* DECEMBER *in the year of our Lord one thousand nine hundred and* FORTY-FIVE *, and of the Independence of the United States of America the one hundred and* SEVENTIETH *.*

By the President:

Adjutant General.

W. D., A. G. O. FORM No. 0650 C.
AUGUST 1, 1938

31

~

"You people are stupid!" The commanding officer bellowed at Mac and his fellow recruits. He had the meanest, coldest blue eyes ever. His uniform was immaculately pressed. "You're recruits until you prove yourself, each and every one of you!" he continued in an icy, menacing manner. "Move your arses out of here!" Mac was not in any place to disagree. Being humiliated and berated was second nature in their training. Demeaning recruits' mothers and sisters was intended to turn them into men who could look a person in the eye and squeeze a trigger. Each grueling day of training ended with "Taps" at night. The cruel and senseless harassment was planned to break them down, put them in good stead later when they confronted an impossible situation in combat. Training enforced responses to orders, not allowing fear to get a grip.

Exhausted each night, Mac fell onto his bunk and missed his mother. He missed Irene even more. He could fall asleep but the

"It's a sound I've always loved—the patter of rain on a tin roof"

			02065506
			02065507
			02065508
			02065509
			02065510
			02065511
			02065512
			02065513
			02065514
			02065515
			02065516
			02065517
			02065518
			02065519
			02065520
			02065521
			02065522
			02065523
BRADLEY, JOHN H., JR	02065488	EISENBROWER, ROWLAND E.	02065524
BASON, WILLIAM A.	02065489	ENGEL, HERMAN, JR	02065525
BAUTZ, JOHN J., JR	02065490	FELDMAN, HOWARD U.	02065526
BELKNAP, NORTON	02065491	FIRESTEIN, ABRAHAM J.Z.	02065527
BERMAN, SANFORD	02065492	FLEMING, DAVID D.	02065528
BERTLEY, CHRIS	02065493	FORBES, ROBIN W.	02065529
BETTNER, JOHN A.	02065494	FOSTER, KENDALL E.	02065530
BODDY, RONALD D.	02065495	FRECHETTE, ARTHUR J., JR	02065531
BOLEY, WILLIAM S.	02065496	FREEMAN, GEORGE N.	02065532
BOMGARDNER, WILLIAM E.	02065497	FRIEDLANDER, GILBERT A.	02065533
BONAPARTE, ROBERT L.	02065498	GANDOLFI, GINO A.	02065534
BOOTH, DOUGLAS Y.	02065499	GERSHOWITZ, JACK	02065535
BOTTOMLEY, THOMAS A.,JR	02065500	GLOVER, WORLEY F.	02065536
BOW, RONALD T.	02065501	GOLDBERG, NATHANIEL E.	02065537
BRISBIN, JACK W.	02065502	GOLDSTEIN, KENNETH K.	02065538
BRUBAKER, ROBERT E.	02065503	GOOTLIEB, GERALD	02065539
BRUMMER, LAWRENCE H.	02065504	GREGG, ROBERT L.	02065540
BUCHANAN, THOMAS E.	02065505	GRIFFITHS, JAMES C.	02065541

(1)

33

anxiety woke him up. As he was absorbing the training to not care about his mother and sweetheart back home, he still missed them.

In Texas, Mac learned to parachute and to play an ocarina. Flying miles above the ground, he and the other trainees jumped into the clouds in a sunny, warm sky until he didn't think about it much. He'd jump, count from one-one-thousand to ten-one-thousand, pull the cord, then enjoy the view parachuting down. The aviation cadets graduated from flight school on August 7th, 1944 with a crisp and orderly ceremony.

~

Sq' Bik' ego Na'ada' "We live in accordance with the stars."— Navajo saying

"When all the stars were ready to be placed in the sky First Woman said, I will use these to write the laws that are to govern mankind for all time. These laws cannot be written on the water as that is always changing its form, nor can they be written in the sand as the wind would soon erase them, but if they are written in the stars they can be read and remembered forever."'—Franc Johnson Newcomb

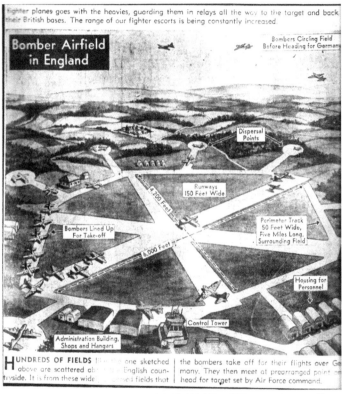

fighter planes goes with the heavies, guarding them in relays all the way to the target and back their British bases. The range of our fighter escorts is being constantly increased.

Bomber Airfield in England

Bombers Circling Field Before Heading for Germany

Dispersal Points

Runways 150 Feet Wide

4,200 Feet

Bombers Lined Up For Take-off

Perimeter Track 50 Feet Wide, Five Miles Long, Surrounding Field

6,000 Feet

Housing for Personnel

Control Tower

Administration Building, Shops and Hangars

HUNDREDS OF FIELDS like the one sketched above are scattered about the English countryside. It is from these wide spread fields that | the bombers take off for their flights over Germany. They then meet at prearranged points and head for target set by Air Force command.

The Cost of Bombing Germany

If 50 Bombers Are Lost— On a 1,000-plane Operation, It Represents—

$15,000,000 In Planes.

$17,500,000 In Crew Training (500 Men)

These costs do not include wear and tear on planes, construction of airfields, training of vast army of mechanics and specialists, and other things necessary in launching major attacks against Germany.

In each major attack the U.S. Air Force launches from Britain, a half billion dollars worth of Air Power goes into action. A 2,000-Plane raid would cost approximately—

1000 Bombers $300,000,000	1000 Fighters $75,000,000
2,500 Tons of Bombs $12,000,000	5,000 Tons of Gasoline $750,000
Training of 11,000 Men $385,000,000	[Ten men to each bomber, one pilot to a fighter at an average of $35,000 per man.]

Comparative Losses— In 13 major assaults during the recent blitz beginning Feb. 19—

ALLIED LOSSES
287 Bombers 37 Fighters

GERMAN LOSSES
644 Fighters

[Each symbol represents 25 planes]

THIS CHART shows the dollars and cents cost to train crew members and maintenance men, to build the planes and furnish the supplies that go to make up one of the giant raids which have | been striking the enemy with increasing frequency in recent weeks. Chart at the left is based on 5 per cent bomber loss, which is considered average.

MAP AND CHARTS BY TOM F. BARRETT OF SUN STAFF.

1944 Jesus, Mary and Joseph, Molesworth England

After transport by boats, buses and trains, Mac was stationed, in November 1944, at Molesworth, England, north of Cambridge, to navigate B-17 bomber missions over Germany. Each mission morning began with a careful dressing in a certain order. First, he patted his lucky charm, a photo of Irene. He shaved with a choice: peering at himself in a broken piece of mirror in which he could only see part of his face, or at a shield of reflective metal where he could just barely see all of his face. He donned a pressed uniform shirt and slacks, with belt, that he had laid out the night before. Polished boots were last, the laces tautly tied.

Dawn barely showed in the misty rain on the tarmac. It took guts to start up the ignition of a plane filled with gasoline and packed with bombs. Ten planes lifted off into close-flying formations. Squadrons flew mission after mission into the breathless hazards of the morning sky. Mac's plane skimmed over a gliding sea far below. Rising sunlight glinted off the tips of patterned whitecaps. Tips or hulls of dark ship carcasses, some with smoky plumes, interrupted the repeated glistening pattern of wind and waves. It wasn't long before he could get a glimpse of Belgium along the horizon. His interphone crackled.

"Pilots, check status."

"Set," the co-pilot replied. "Set" was repeated by each crew member.

Two small aircraft lined the target. The bombardier counted to twenty. The lead bomber dropped his load on the strategic witch-hat shapes that loomed below in stone. Eleven other planes unloaded incendiaries. Strangers on the ground swore back in German, shot at them with cannons of exploding flak. A blackened cloud of rounded metal-like feathers dropped at the same diagonal. Forty bombs per plane. Ten planes, seventy-two thousand pounds of explosives, were downed.

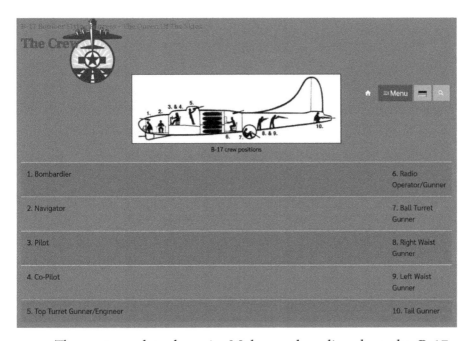

1. Bombardier	6. Radio Operator/Gunner
2. Navigator	7. Ball Turret Gunner
3. Pilot	8. Right Waist Gunner
4. Co-Pilot	9. Left Waist Gunner
5. Top Turret Gunner/Engineer	10. Tail Gunner

They returned to base in Molesworth, relieved as the B-17 returned to base camp. They'd defied the angel of death again. The time spent waiting in between missions was worse than the flights. Each successful brush with death brought everything to life; the smell of grass and burnt fuel, the soil and singed rubber, the asphalt and hollyhocks.

~

"We wanted to be goodness and decency in all that evil," Dad said. "We wanted to be for justice and courtesy. We were eager to be good men." My pen flew as I jotted his reflections in the pauses between reading. In England, he'd recognized the colors again in the winter, reddish roofs slated with blues, Payne's gray plumes rising from red chimneys. What was treasured became crystal clear. The sunset became worthy of study, and capturing each and every streak and pink-lined cloud in a dark world. Dad wanted to be his best, part of the best of the world.

~

On both sides of the ever-changing boundaries during the war, young men risked their lives for what they were told was their country's pride. The Catch-22 was they were being shot at on each mission. They also had to complete a number of missions to get sent home. Mac navigated through screeching and whistling shells exploding all around him in the clear plastic nose of a B-17. He wondered if his youth had come to an end. He missed Irene.

Every five missions, Mac would get a three-day pass. He spent time with a friend, Curley, a British flyer. Mac and Curley kept themselves occupied in London, with theatre, movies and dinner. Curley invited Mac to his family home for dinners, a welcome distraction. Not that he complained, but Mac's visits to Curley's home were not for the British cuisine. Curley's family scrimped their rations for their formal meals. They prepared for their son and his American friend slices of melon drizzled with cherry glaze served in silver dishes over candle-heated plate warmers. Slices of tough roast beef swam in thickened gravy with mushy, overcooked vegetables and bluish potatoes; potatoes were

always served. The rosé wine came from French regions with no labels. Mac relaxed when Curley's mother hovered over the dishes, as she reminded him of being home with his own mother. Mac and Curley kept each other's humor up and Mac was invited often.

~

Dawn barely showed in the misty rain on the tarmac.

"Pilots, man your planes!" blared over the speaker.

Mac blazed through his 13th, 14th, then 15th missions. Fear crept in. *When did the vertigo set in? From the constant migration across the eastern U.S. with changing labels: Navy Officer; Army Corpsman; 2nd Lieutenant; Commander; dog tags: 0 2065589; Pilot; Navigator; 303rd Bomber Squad? From flying five miles above ground in frozen air? From the sleep-deprived dream state of unpressurized cabins?* The lucky ones finished fifty missions, black flak nightmares. It changed to sixty missions.

While Mac carefully counted aerial missions that December of 1944, Germany reared its deadliest, most desperate attempt to split the Allied Armies. A quarter-million troops, of a triad *blitzkrieg*, marched Ardennes frozen forests. Allied planes were ordered grounded in bad weather.

Everything for Mac's fifteenth mission went as planned. The German *Luftwaffe* was nearly defeated. Allied planes roamed at will.

~

On Mac's sixteenth mission, he was awakened by a hurried, hushed conversation talking down a crazed airman. It reminded him of his training, *Keep your wits about you*. His muscles tightened remembering one flight in particular. He'd nearly passed out when his goggles slid under an edge of his oxygen mask. Woozy and in a panic, he was able to shift his mask in time and regained his equilibrium.

Mac's mission was with the 303rd Bomb Group of the 8th Airforce in a plane called "Red." They were assigned to fly to Mannheim and take over for a visual bomb run. The operation was abruptly canceled, and Mac exhaled. On standby, he got to know his new crew. He chatted with the co-pilot, John "Tex" Cornyn, over a new-fangled helicopter that was parked on the tarmac.

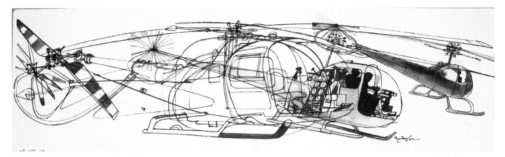

"That silly-looking whirly gig of a piece of equipment couldn't possibly fly," Mac said. He laughed. "I'm never going up in one of those."

"I'm rather curious to fly it," Cornyn said. Inspired by Cornyn's open mind, Mac later sketched the helicopter for a painting.

The mission was reinstated, and Mac inhaled.

~

In the bomber, ten men in heavy leather jackets with fleece lining, electric suits and boots prepared for takeoff. Tex began the call-in:

"Bomb bays, in the middle."

"Set!" A catwalk between the bombs would later open behind the raised flight deck.

"Bombardier."

"Set!" The bombardier looked through a Norden bombsight to calculate the bomb drop over the target and fly the plane on autopilot.

"Engineer."

"Set!" The engineer stood above in the Plexiglas bubble on top.

"Waist gunners."

"Set!" Two gunners fired from both sides of the open bays mid-plane as frigid air blew in.

"Radio operator."

"Set!" The operator sat at a table next to the small blister window behind the bomb bay.

A Plexiglas sphere was underneath the belly, installed with two .50 caliber machine guns and one small-framed, nimble man.

"Short ball gunner."

"Set!" This gunner revolved like a fetus in a womb tracking fighter planes below with spiraling rapid fire. Without hydraulic power, he could be locked in his bubble. He was responsible for defending the bottom of the plane if the Axis fighters attacked from underneath, but the Germans typically flew high out from the sun.

"Tail gunner."

"Set!" The Tail Gunner position lined the fuselage, the loneliest position on the plane.

"Navigator."

"Set!" Mac plugged his suit into an outlet on the inner wall of the unheated plane. He suddenly worried about his suit; heated suits could short out and burn its wearer. Mac's worry then shifted to the intersecting runways as their plane lined up for takeoff.

For courage, they sang:

"Off we go into the wild blue yonder, climbing high into the sun… We live in fame, or go down in flames… Hey! Nothing'll stop the Army Air Corps!"

Red blasted off down the bumpy runway. Four-engine planes ascended, spiraling into tight box formation for maximum mutual protection at a slow climb to a five-mile height. It took hours to get into formation, and not all crews survived it. No matter what, they had to stay in formation. Often, Mac navigated while blinded by a vapor trail.

~

After flying low over the glistening North Sea, Red's crew donned oxygen masks and earphones as they climbed to frigid heights of ten thousand feet. After the squadron reached the initial point, the lead B-17 turned towards the target. All bombardiers shifted into alertness. They counted to twenty. The lead plane dropped its bombs. Then, the planes behind dropped theirs. The sky blackened with bombs like broken rosary beads falling downward.

Precision bombing often missed, some by a long shot. American precision bombing only happened in daylight, which caused huge losses of airplanes and men. One plane in formation exploded. Another fell into a tailspin, righted itself and turned back to base. Flak shells burst all around.

Fatigue set in and the cold was exhausting. Red drew closer to the target and exploded flak was everywhere. Mac could smell the black oily-looking puffs in the air. Bursts of explosions surrounded their plane and shrapnel pierced the thin metal. *Thunk!*

Mac heard steely calm voices from above and below over the interphone.

"Set!" Mac called back.

Outside, another plane, Dottie, went down in flames.

The head squadron banked and Red prepared to drop but not before catching more flak from enemy fire. Shells lit up with an eerie green light in the falling snow. The formation continued to drop, then turned.

"The target is near!" shouted the bombardier. He counted down over the interphone, then shouted, "Bombs Away!"

~

Red was hit in the bomb bay. Smoke filled the plane. The instrument panel was covered with smoke and frost. The pilot, Jack Rose, turned Red out of formation. Anoxia took effect. Fatigue and exhaustion permeated the crew. Mac remembered his training: *Breathe, relax, keep your wits about you.* Red took a hit under the chin turret. Ammunition exploded. Smoke and howling wind filled the cockpit. Flake Dyson, the engineer, was blown out of the fuselage and from the turret position, ending up between Rose and Tex in the cockpit. Then came the worst hit—behind engine Number Four.

The first warning bell rang. Chutes were grabbed. Flak suits were removed. The explosions were deafening even with the headphones. Back in his seat, Mac was tying his boot when the plane went into a tailspin. He found himself face down, spinning against his harness straps. *Keep your wits about you. Our Father, who art in heaven, hallowed be thy name...*

"Throttling Engine One and Engine Two!" Rose shouted.

"Copy that!" Tex said.

The centrifugal force pinned everyone down; no one could parachute out. Rose throttled back on Engines One and Two. Red righted itself. Mac exhaled with relief.

"Navigator!" came over the interphone.

"Set!" Mac shouted.

Mac reached for his instruments to calculate a new heading. *We might make it! If only the fire blows out, we might make it!* Rose's voice came over the interphone again.

"Red is not responding to controls!" Rose shouted. There was an ominous pause, then, "Prepare to bail out."

~

Fire closed in on Mac's part of the plane. As he prepared to exit, his training kicked in—Mac folded up a silk map of Germany and tucked it up his sleeve. He then reached for his most precious possession, a photo of Irene, which he tucked in with the map.

Mac saw Rose, Cornyn, Dyson and the waist gunners approaching through the smoke. Rose waved him on.

"Navigator jumps first!"

Mac thought about Irene as he left his .45 pistol in the desk. *I'm not going to shoot my way out of Germany.*

Mac kicked out the escape hatch near his station. He looked down through the smoke and clouds four miles above the forest. *The fire, the explosions, lack of oxygen, the guys behind, God!* Mac jumped.

"Jesus, Mary and Joseph, spare me!" His cry exploded in subzero air.

~

Mac gasped a thin breath of frozen air, a two-hundred-mile-per-hour *Whoosh*. He fought against passing out. Mac found himself in a free fall amidst exploding flak.

"One-one-thousand." Shrapnel sliced at Mac's coat and face. "Two-one-thousand." Blood froze. "Three-one-thousand." Tears froze. "Four-one-thousand."

Mac's mind raced. *Focus on the D-ring. Did the guy pack this chute right? Need oxygen... Don't pass out. Focus.* "Five-one-thousand." *Guys free fall 10,000 feet for oxygen. Don't wait. Got to know if this will open. Clear Red.* "Six one-thousand, seven-one-thousand... eight-one thousand." *Pull the D-ring!*

The parachute unraveled in Mac's face, hitting his nose, cheeks and ears. A tremendous jolt stopped Mac short amidst exploding flak. He passed out.

~

Time passed slowly. Mac awoke and found himself floating with muffled detonations in the distance. *Get your wits together.* He pulled on the parachute's shroud lines to guide his landing. He noticed that his boot was missing. *Foot is frozen. No boot! No sock! Keep your wits!*

Mac descended through icy smoke. He smelled scorched metal, then wafts of farm manure. Winter forests and frozen streams outlined the Earth in a burst of evergreen and stone gray. Hearth fires from tiny houses triggered Mac's longing for home. He shed tears of relief and a strange joy as vague memories of warmth and food flooded his mind. He imagined that a stew was being cooked in the village.

~

January 13th, 1945. Pirmasens, Germany

Mac landed in broad daylight in a snowy soccer field. Citizens, police, kids and stray dogs saw him, and he saw them. They ran towards him shouting *"Terrorflieger!"* A "terror flyer." Frozen and scared, Mac struggled to release the parachute harness then sprinted with one wet foot. Woozy, Mac scrambled up a hill. *Fast through the snow... Hide. There's a cave. They're not following.*

In the cave, Mac ripped the inside of his jacket sleeve and stuffed the silk map and photo up higher behind his elbow. He knew that German propaganda ministers dropped leaflets from planes through the streets alerting civilians to report "any Allied air force soldiers." If caught by citizens, they might pull Mac apart limb from limb. *Keep your wits about you. Wait for the guards.* German soldiers arrived and Mac was hauled away.

~

Mac was marched past a red brick town hall with a towering clock. Soldiers who captured an officer knew their job was to get their prisoner to an interrogator. The soldiers barked commands in German, escalating Mac's fear.

The Germans had also captured co-pilots Jack Rose and John Cornyn. Cornyn's .45 pistol was confiscated by a *Hauptmann*, a Captain, an imposing figure.

"Gangster pistol," he said with a heavy accent.

Only one of Red's airmen—also captured—spoke German. On the plane, he had listened to the radio and told others what the broadcasts were saying. He told Mac that the airmen were considered

Kriegsgefangeners, prisoners of war. After Red was crippled and flaming, Cornyn had decided to ditch the plane. One guy jumped, then another, then another. They landed spread out in various clearings or outcroppings. Two or three were captured nearby. None of them showed recognition of each other.

The POWs were marched through Bavarian-styled blocks of buildings on cobbled sidewalks of various colored four-story homes. Mac looked all around. Led by rifles in single file past medieval Romer and St. Nicholas Church, Mac felt the depth of history, a thousand year-old architecture.

In front of an armed guard, Mac didn't acknowledge his fellow airmen, nor did they show him recognition as they were marched through the center of the once medieval city center leveled by bombs. Trees were ripped to splintered shards next to crumbled stones with low walls that were once homes. A horrified pit rose in Mac's stomach. *What was this war? Why are we here?* No one showed any emotion. None of the prisoners talked to each other. Leafless trees and trunks were black with wet snow. The roads were cleared of cars and pedestrians for jeeps, troops, POWs and artillery to move through. Mac remembered what H.G. Wells had written of what a tank might look like. "In that flickering pallor, it had the effect of a large and clumsy black insect, an insect the size of an ironclad cruiser, crawling obliquely to the first line of trenches and firing shots out of portholes in its side." Not fear of the Third Reich, nothing, prepared Mac for the imposing Tiger Tanks as they rolled between beamed, double gables with colored stucco. Giant turret guns tipped into the sky from sleek, precision killing-machines on rotating tracks. Mac was awestruck.

~

Red's crew was transported into Frankfurt by train and then by tram to nearby *Durchgangslager der Luftwaffe* or *Luftwaffe Dulag Luft,* for collection. From previous bombings, framework metal was twisted and shards of glass fell from the canopy onto platforms and tracks. Angry civilians shouted, *"Luftgangster!"* ("Gangster") and "Murderer" in German and English. Outside, troops of German soldiers marched in unison, like automatons, down what was left of the cobblestone streets. Expressionless German soldiers marched in step; the loud, steady rhythm of boots rained down heavily on hard stones. Everything about them gleamed: buttons, boots, those metal coal-scuttled hats. Their blank stares were scarier than the rifles slung over their shoulders.

Mac and the crew were transported via a twenty-minute tram to Oberusel. After being given his new ID card and fingerprinted, Mac was put into a tiny six-feet by six-feet cement cell with fleas for company. At Auswertestelle West, the Interrogation and Evaluation Center, interrogations were carried out: temperature fluctuations and solitary confinement. The air carried the odor of a pail in the corner of the cell that served as a bathroom. A small opaque window, never opened, allow almost no light. Only a single lightbulb hung from the ceiling and burned day and night. Exhausted, the men slept fitfully on straw mattresses. Meager meals were delivered by German staff. From time to time, they were taken to an interrogator, who spoke perfect English and greeted them warmly. In the meantime, Mac paced three feet back and forth with his shoeless foot colder than the other. He wore the same clothes he had been shot down in, and that would not change for many weeks.

Guards clicked the heat on and "forgot" it was on; the cells were extremely hot for hours before they switched it off again. Mac learned that this was the *Luftwaffe*, not the SS, the hated "rival." *Luftwaffe* interrogators were "polite," and in the early days, they took some POWs to the local bar, for walks in the mountains and even called home for some of them. The master interrogator there used a particular form of "kindness" rather than torture to get what he wanted.

Mac stomped about in his cell as he grappled with the moral complexities of war. *Holy Mary, Mother of God. Pray for our sins...* Mac mentally listed his belongings: one boot, the map, a blanket, an empty canteen, his coat, his pants, his prayers. *POW 9324 William F. McMahon, 2nd Lieutenant of the Army Air Corp, 02065589.* Name, rank and serial number were all they would get from him.

~

Generals called this a war of nerves. Guards tried to make Mac uncomfortable. The nuns at his childhood St. Itas entered his consciousness, repeating, *"Do not kill."* The "etiquette" of war didn't make sense to Mac. He had not fired a shot at a person. *Was I excused in God's eyes from murder? What was war about?* Anger arose within Mac. *Everyone at home is comfortable. Why am I here alone, trapped, hungry?*

With an imaginary pencil, Mac captured the look, the likeness, that strange wildness in his guard's eyes. *Draw it again.* Thickness to thinness of line gave depth to nostrils, eye corners, ears. This kept

the committee of a thousand voices and fears at bay. Mac sketched for a tomorrow he could not yet see. Strength, purpose and true faith emerged from those dark shadows by tracing likenesses in his memory. In between interrogations Mac gathered more details for mind-drawing. He checked his proportions. Insights into gestures and expressions kept him observing intently. The drawing gave a purpose to his unearthly hell.

~

The cell door rattled open and a guard took Mac to be interrogated. He was greeted with, "Come in, I am your interrogator," by a tall man in an immaculate blue *Luftwaffe* uniform. He spoke perfect English, having lived in the U.S. before the war. He offered Mac a cigarette and smoked one himself. He spread out folders and papers on his desk. Mac sat across from him in a chair.

The interrogator knew about the plane, Red, where it crashed and more facts about Red's crew than Mac knew. He knew Mac's mother's name, where he went to high school, and where the military trained him. His questions to Mac were answered with only Mac's name, rank, and serial number. Mac had to hide his astonishment at what the man knew and how he knew it.

"What was your target?" the interrogator asked. "What kind of bombs were you carrying? What do you know about the Norden bombsight?"

Mac was not forthcoming, so he was returned to his cell.

~

Back in his cell, Mac made images with no pencil or paper; it organized and calmed his mind. Unlike most men who looked outward, Mac had a way of looking inward to reflect the impressions that this astonishing world flung upon him. He was determined to look closer and closer at his surroundings, then reflect as he processed an impression of himself from within.

Dulag Luft days tested Mac's hard-earned endurance. He had parachuted into a place at the bottom of Dante's Inferno, to the bottom of life itself. Repetition in tasks made a new world order. Then he was taken to his interrogator again.

"Why are you fighting against Germany? You should not even be in this war."

Name rank and serial number—careful. After a few more "soft" interrogations, a guard arrived to take Mac to the transition center where he joined other prisoners who had finished their interrogations. The Red Cross served a hot meal. Mac was able to shower and sleep in a bed.

Mac was presented his first Red Cross Packet parcel that was eaten before he left the center. He and Red's crewmembers were marched to the train station with over a hundred other prisoners for a three-day train trip to Stalag Luft III in Sagan. At the train station, they parted with their enlisted waist gunner, who was sent to an enlisted men's camp.

They took the tram to the Frankfurt train station, where Hitler Youth sang spirited marching songs until they saw the airmen and started yelling lewd obscenities with all the hatred they could rally.

The air raid siren blasted the icy air. The officer-prisoners were strong-armed into a bomb shelter by guards. Allied planes dropped their payload. Screaming avalanches shadowed the terrified crowd racing for cover. The station shook and glass shattered. Explosions pierced eardrums. Walls vibrated and crumbled and Mac looked upward. *We could be buried alive!* Screams, moans, howls and sobs erupted then, and roaring loudness reverberated. Furious, panicked, civilians dove into the shelter. The *kriegies* were tightly cramped with the Germans. Not every German felt good about Hitler, but hatred for Allied airmen fueled the villagers' stares directed at the American troublemakers. Mac squirmed. Everything was inaudible. His eyes

adjusted to the dark, and he glanced about, momentarily deaf, but aware.

An indigo-eyed nine-year-old boy in a Hitler Youth uniform stared at Mac. A row of stoic, uniformed boys, one straw-blonde with sapphire eyes, one white-blond with azure eyes, a cerulean-eyed platinum blonde and another with sandy hair and cyan eyes sat on a bench. The boys shared his anxiety. They shared the silence. No one could hear.

Mac found being a *kriegie* demoralizing. An overwhelming hopelessness settled in his heart. At first, it was easy for Mac to sit back and follow orders. The "promise" of survival numbed any instinct to escape. The captors kept a close eye on their prized officers, each a potential fount of information. The prodding, poking and commanding resumed when the air raid siren went silent. The boys were harshly commanded to leave their shelter first. One spit at

the *kriegies*. Citizens were directed to leave next. Prisoners were then prodded by pointy rifles.

~

Mac arrived at Sagan station in Poland. His eyes took time to adjust to the gray clouded haze of light. They filed past a tall lean brick guard house where their IDs were checked. They slogged up a sandy road for a quarter mile to the camp. Mac could smell the pine trees.

Mac got a view of the camp as he passed the ten-foot rustic fence made of split pine saplings nailed closely together leading ahead to the main gate. A huge sign emblazoned with a black *swastika* hung limply from a pole near the *Vorlager*, the German administrative building, a small hospital, and a cooler at the camp's entrance. Through an enormous gate on his left, Mac could see clusters of green-gray weathered barracks, a barbed wire fence and elevated wooden guard towers. Stumpy trunks sat between the maze of barbed wire between compounds and the forest.

Guards swung open the gate and peremptorily checked papers. The cluster of men were paraded through with low spirits as the gate shut abruptly behind them. Warily, Mac looked around

HEADQUARTERS
303 RD BOMBARDMENT GROUP (H)
APO # 557, c/o POSTMASTER
NEW YORK CITY, NEW YORK.

January 14, 1944.

Mrs. Elizabeth F. Mc Mahon,
22 Banks,
Chicago, Ill.

Dear Mrs. Mc Mahon:

On behalf of the Commanding General of the Eighth Air Force and the Commanding Officer of the 303rd Bombardment Group (H), I wish to express the deep sympathy the personnel of the 303rd Bombardment Group (H) feel for you at the loss of your son, 2nd Lt. William F. Mc Mahon, O2065589, who has been missing in action since January 13, 1944.

I sincerely regret that I can give you no additional information about your son. I can assure you, however, that as soon as definite information is available, the War Department will immediately notify you. Although I can appreciate the fact that you are anxious for some word, any word, there is nothing I can say which would not be pure conjecture.

Certainly words are inadequate to express our sympathy, but we do want you to know that all of us are deeply touched by the sudden loss of our friend and comrade. We pray for you that God may give you much courage to go through these trying days; that He may provide comfort in your hours of trial. We who knew and lived with your son, will never give up hope for him, but place our faith in the compassion of a just and righteous Almighty God.

Very sincerely yours,

Edmund J. Skoner,
Chaplain.

at his compound, three hundred yards square with two fences about ten feet high and five feet apart around it. Each fence was strung with twenty closed strands of rusted barbed wire. About fifty yards behind the fences stood the "goon-boxes" on stilts fifteen feet high, with guards at the top with search lights, machine guns and phones. German guards pointed their weapons from towers in greeting. Thirty feet inside the barbed wire was a warning wire about eighteen inches high. Everything was gray. Gray earth and aged barracks, gray clothes and worn floors.

New prisoners were herded into the forecourt of a stark building. The men were led in one-by-one for processing, ID card check, and given a square metal identification tag stamped "Stalag Luft III" and a POW number. They were then taken to a leader and marched through ten-feet-high double barbed wire fences to the West compound and told to find a place to live.

The men were deloused and then showered from a Nescafe can punched with holes over a cold-water pipe. Mac was issued bedding—a thin wool blanket, one sheet, one mattress filled with wood shavings, one pillowcase, one small linen towel and one pillow filled with straw. Also, a two-quart mixing bowl, one cup, knife, fork, spoon, given once and would not be replaced. Mac was handed a paper package with a bar of soap, razor, cup, bowl and spoon, all tied with a cotton string in a knot. The silk map was still in his sleeve, and his clothes—minus one boot, was his list of items owned. Everything was a shade of gray as if a veil had dropped over the colors of the world. Mac unwrapped the paper, coiled the string and put both in his pocket.

Kriegies were called to attention. A *Luftwaffe* officer strutted over to welcome them with an American service officer who then led them off for a talk in a theater for a one-hour briefing on how the camp was organized, its activities, and regulations. Current prisoners pooled their Red Cross parcel items to augment feeding incoming men, knowing their deprivations. Within a couple of hours, Mac learned that the wire contained French, British, Australian, South African, New Zealander, Canadian and Yank *Kriegies*. Only Americans were in West Compound. Wary Americans tested Mac with history and sports trivia to ensure he wasn't a German spy in their barracks.

Mac tossed his mattress and pillow on the wooden bunk. It was more of a wooden shelf built four-by-four, three platforms high. The corner stove was not enough to warm the barracks. That first night, with the stove flickering, he considered what he'd become in two short weeks. *Will my foot fester with infection? Heimweh* was the German word for longing for one's home.

~

Mac was the guy with the new map. *Germany is beautiful, but I live in gray*. He teared up as he sat to write a letter to his mother that he was in good shape and in a POW camp. Often, he stopped to rub his sore shoulder and counted his blessings. "So, I'm in the bag," Mac said as he set down his belongings on a middle bunk.

"Hey, do you have a smoke?"

The question came from Barney, who sat on the next bunk. No one sat on another's bunk. Four slats were taken out of Mac's bunk to shore up tunnels dug in sandy Silesian soil. Barney was too thin, scruffily shaven under his hawk-beak nose, crumpled posture and draped clothing. Through Barney, Mac realized journalism was replaced by the twins: Gossip and Rumor. Barney's idle chatter of loosely-composed factless statements enhanced his feeling of skidding on a slippery slope. Overheard conversations from a guard or colonel, often of German propaganda, were negated in a constant chatter or accepted as fact by Barney. Gossip and Rumor dialogued on with no protagonist, plot or characters. Barney could weave a tale that kept the frozen air moving. Moments were small and sentences were short, each an infinitesimal piece of a very great—or very small —world at war.

"*Ruhe, Ruhe!*" They were ordered quiet. Mac didn't comprehend the perpetually impatient shouted orders. He remained quiet.

~

"Hey, do you have a smoke?" Barney asked a guy by the fire. No one ever did. The prisoners received tons of cigarettes in Red Cross parcels every two weeks, but Mac did not smoke. He saw how Barney traded the solids in his soup for cigarettes.

Mac convinced himself to be content. *Will my heart work again?* Settling his head on his small pillow, Mac dozed into a bitter and rigid sleep under a thin wool blanket. Strained and spent, he dozed into abrupt awakenings. Nightmares of the dead floated up to the planes to wrap arms around Red's nose. He talked to his mother in his sleep, but she couldn't hear him and was indifferent. *Indifference was more painful than hate.* She floated away without a word. *Am I asleep or awake?* Mac gazed out intently to see if the dreamt figure was still there. He felt sick from his flak-filled dreams. A frosty cry went out from the bunks. Then a sleepy laugh. Someone else was snoring puffs of cold vapor. Another talked loudly in his sleep and sobbed uncontrollably. No one shushed him, no one consoled him.

Mac cleared his mind of the dream. He wished to dream in color, but everything was a foggy cold gray. Nightmares of hungry, fatigued sleepwalkers returned from nowhere, bathed in the eerie green light of a florescent aquarium behind melting glass. The blankets were not long enough or warm enough. A distant owl hooted. Mac slept.

~

I found documentation in my mother's boxes of Gramma Mac's search for her son. No news of MIA Army Air Corps, 02065589 for a month. Gramma melted in relief when two Army officers knocked on her door. On January 10th, Mac sent a telegram to his mother, at her new 10 W. Elm home.

"I've gone to the theater with Curley in London." On March 23rd, a second telegram arrived on Elm, thanking Bess Franklin McMahon for her Red Cross notice of P.O.W. W.F. McMahon, Army Air Corps, 02065589, a POW in good health.

~

Kriegies were called to attention as a *Luftwaffe* officer walked in to welcome them with the American service officer who led them off for a talk in the theater. Mac perked up when a counter of art YWCA art supplies was mentioned. Mac and the others were marched to the mess hall for German rations.

~

Aufstechen! Like a stone, the foreign command fell to the bottom of Mac's soul. Chilled gusts of winter blew into his Silesian barrack. The illusion of a warm blanket and night's sleep shattered around him. He wiped his boot in an everlasting cold. His hair was brushed by fingers, long strands of hair catching in his cuticles. He shaved every day as best as he could. Baring his cheeks to the insult of a daily routine with a dull razor drawn by his degraded exhaustion of spirit, Mac confronted an atrocious and vulnerable nakedness of survival each morning. Stroke by stroke, his razor cut through the night's stubble and a human emerged. He turned and faced the dusty opaque cloud of a grumbling barrack.

~

Only those who worked received anything above subsistence rations. Officers did no work so could not expect a working man's rations. The German diet was one ration per week: potatoes wheat, barley, rye, sawdust brown bread (each loaf weighed 4.5 lbs), cabbage, *ersatz* margarine, marmalade, but never meat. Mac learned to eat to live rather than live to eat, with his heart melting as he spread Red Cross orange marmalade over torn bread slabs. Bread seemed huge in another's hand; his own, tiny enough to make him quiver. If he traded his rations, the illusion was inverted: his portion was undersized and the other was generous. *Guys slap bread against the stove? Those Germans can't believe we'd toast bread.* Barney had some nincompoop story going about a guard and his gal that captured some attention. It continued all the way to the latrines. Dawn offered glimmers of color. Distant artillery explosions looked like summer heat lightning with no thunder. Rumbles reverberated over the hills, then shots were heard nearby.

Mac maintained an aura of mystery about himself; that way, he wasn't pounced on by the guards and searched. He kept his sensitivity to the human condition alive by seeing into his captors. He stayed clean and orderly, implied he would be above escape. He earned freedom from being closely watched.

"Ya' frickin' Mac?" whispered a seasoned POW who bumped his shoulder during barracks check.

"I'm Mac, why?" His mouth was dry from not speaking.

"Don't ask, just meet me at the last goddamned lunch table on the right... And bring your frickin' map."

Long, morning train whistles wailed through the bare trees and waning dawn from the valley below. A lingering line formed out the unlocked splintered door for breakfast.

"Foocking shut the door, it's freezing in here!" Lunch was soup, a big bucket of soup. POWs shouted, "Frickin' stir it up!" to get some of the solids to float up. In line, Barney stood close when another guy lit up a cigarette to breathe in the airborne smoke.

"Flick off!" Guys didn't share cigarettes. Barney waited, hoping for a puff. He traded his solid vegetables for cigarettes. When he couldn't get a smoke, he traded more solids from his soup. Mac looked for the last table on the right. *Barney's wasting away.* There was no radiance in that soup line. At best, all eyes were infused with a wildness, a fatigued survival. All eyes seemed to emit an acquired sorrow. A quick glance up above a soup bowl let Mac know he'd gotten to the right bench.

"So, you know how to frickin' draw?" The question was whispered to the soup bowl.

"Yeah, cartoons mostly," Mac answered.

"Hand over the frickin' map. Cassie will show you the ropes and give you some work."

"I need my map," he stated.

"Just give us the frickin' map. You'll get it back, if you're lucky."

"Okay, I want my map back," Mac repeated. "Do you have an extra left boot? Size nine."

"We'll get you a frickin' boot, just give us the frickin' map."

"And a sock."

Mac was welcomed into the smoke-filled room of the underground political system that had been organized into an intricate pattern of patronage and cunning. He handed over his silk map to an underground of defiance and survival organized by an international group of leaders. The POWs printed copies of his map in a handmade press, a clothes-washing wooden roller with blanket squares. With a strip of blanket and ink made from fat-lamp black mixed with neat's-foot oil, impressions of Mac's map were transferred. A fair-fitting boot and a sock were dropped off under Mac's bunk. *No laces.*

Barney gabbed about the seventy-six escapees from Stalag Luft III via an elaborate tunnel, civilian clothes and false identifications.

"That's where our slats went—to shore up the sandy tunnel. It took 70,000 police to search and find all but three escapees," Barney said. "Forty-seven of the captured prisoners were shot while taking a piss by the side of a road. Three more were murdered elsewhere." He and Mac fought the biting cold to visit the stone memorial built to honor the fifty murdered escapees from the *Great Escape*, as signed on a cartoon by First Lieutenant Alex Cassie.

Mac became acquainted with Carl Holmstrom, who handed out YMCA art supplies. Mac felt the ripple effect of his actions, adapting to a world divided into separate layers of survival systems. He avoided conflict with his bunkmates with humor over his little clutter of possessions, lined up for soup and bread without complaint. He kindled friendships in French.

Mac found ideas for cartoons, which he sent back to Chicago. The cartoons somehow bypassed the censors. He drew a guard, then another and another. More paper was picked up at the Y-counter. He drew *Kommandants* from the shadows. He escaped into his art, into the created image. His heart and soul relaxed.

~

The outer walls of Stalag III's barracks were doubled years ago, but they failed to contain everything. A half-foot of space behind false walls concealed tools, tin cans, dyed cloth and thread. Primitive shallow tunnels were first dug through the sand. Heavy trucks collapsed the hollows. Tunnels were dug deeper, longer and wider. Steam was seen rising from vents. Air pumps made of milk tins fitted together in tubes connected to canvas bellows. Air was pumped deep underground to sweating nearly-naked diggers. Compasses were manufactured using sewing needles rubbed against a magnet. Forgery studios, cartography shops, printing presses were set up in barracks and disassembled in less than a minute. Hazardous hand injuries from filing for hours or digging in close quarters were life-threatening. Malnutrition slowed the healing of sores.

Mac shaved his pencil tip with a single-sided razor. *Achtung!* Shiny buckles and pistols stomped into the barracks unannounced. A leather gloved hand lifted blankets and loose clothing. Not one scrap of paper was found. Mac's charcoaled sticks were hidden in a hollowed bunk post.

Watchmen sent signals from their positions. The motion of moving a chair, standing up, sitting warned of "ferrets". Guards searched ruthlessly for clandestine acts. Mac's silk map disappeared into this covert system with no clues as to how many copies were given to attempted escapees, but there was no word of captures or executions.

A loss of memory and focus caused prisoners to drift to the extremes of optimism and pessimism in any given moment. Low periods of fatigue reached a dull gray bottom. Washing was pointless from filthy basins, but the act of cleansing with vigor was necessary.

Escape became its own game of survival, espionage and underhanded trickery. Threats from the "goons" of shooting prisoners in the camp kept escape plans vital and constant. Germans in a bunch were goons, but one-on-one, away from their families, Mac thought many looked hungry, naked and defenseless, too. They were stuck between two dark, dreaded places—an isolating hell-of-a-war and fear of the Gestapo. Each ferret, *Kommandant*, POW or guard of Stalag Luft III that Mac came across appeared to have one universal hope, the end of a brutal war. Mac drew their likenesses.

Goons were bribed with Red Cross coffee and chocolate in exchange for train lines and schedule information. Biscuits, brew, cigarettes and sympathies expressed to grumbling guards released names and layouts of towns. Train ticket prices slipped out, maps were drawn in detail. IDs were "borrowed" from the goons' overcoats and returned while they shared a glass of raisin-brewed wine. *What foods were ration-free? What were common women's names?* Thousands of handy hints helped men escape the Third Reich.

Rumor traveled fast of officers selected for solitary confinement and interrogation. Barney spread the tale:

"Did you hear about the fookin' guard who opened the door

and turned a high-pressure water hose on a Yank in solitary? The goddamned guy wasn't strong enough to get up and died frozen to the floor." *Ahh, fifty-fifty chance there's any truth to it.*

Prisoners did everything possible to harass guards. "Been-there-too-long" Brits' humor was pervasive. The wily, ribald Americans remade the game. Young London girls, back home, were growing up with no Daddy-daughter dances or boys to dip pig tails into ink jars. British babies grew up and became teens while their imagined fathers sent home occasional letters. American teens added a rowdy, razzle--dazzle to the raucous atmosphere. Germans were left bewildered.

Stealing, lying and other backhanded tricks waged an undercover, unscrupulous war. Radios received both BBC news and gossip between compounds. Mac overheard that, of the men who had escaped, fifty were murdered by guards because they were too claustrophobic to crawl through a tunnel.

A too-early reveille announced a rose-colored dawn across distant knolls. Mac was awake in his bunk. He wasn't dead, but he wasn't alive. For a few moments at waking, that was when his soul lived. It was better for him to not think of something he loved. *The early bird gets the worm.* Mac jumped up, slipped into his clothes, and tightened the cotton string on his new boot. It snapped. He had grown accustomed to rustling bodies rolling out of wooden cells. The beehive of bunks vibrated. The barracks shook to their foundations as the men frantically hurried to long latrine queues. Blankets shook, raising clouds of malodorous dust.

Mac adjusted paper pads in his jacket. A wayward wire threaded his boot eyelets over its tongue that pinched his arch. He loosened the wire, grateful for a covering over his soggy-socked right foot. His razor, mirror and bar of soap were wrapped in a cloth, his daily count of possessions. Mac stepped into the dawn besieged by barking commands. Mac heard that the Geneva Convention stated that captured troops were to be fed properly.

"If Germany loses the war, Hitler's orders are to shoot you all," the guards said. Barney told Mac about a newly issued order: prisoners are to be chained, except American officers.

bar

WAR DEPARTMENT

THE ADJUTANT GENERAL'S OFFICE

WASHINGTON 25, D. C.

IN REPLY REFER TO:

AG 201 McMahon, William F.
PC-N ETO 027

6 February 1945

Mrs. Elizabeth F. McMahon
22 Banks Street
Chicago, Illinois

Dear Mrs. McMahon:

This letter is to confirm my recent telegram in which you were regretfully informed that your son, Second Lieutenant William F. McMahon, 02065589, has been reported missing in action over Germany since 13 January 1945.

I know that added distress is caused by failure to receive more information or details. Therefore, I wish to assure you that at any time additional information is received it will be transmitted to you without delay, and, if in the meantime no additional information is received, I will again communicate with you at the expiration of three months. Also, it is the policy of the Commanding General of the Army Air Forces upon receipt of the "Missing Air Crew Report" to convey to you any details that might be contained in that report.

The term "missing in action" is used only to indicate that the whereabouts or status of an individual is not immediately known. It is not intended to convey the impression that the case is closed. I wish to emphasize that every effort is exerted continuously to clear up the status of our personnel. Under war conditions this is a difficult task as you must readily realize. Experience has shown that many persons reported missing in action are subsequently reported as prisoners of war, but as this information is furnished by countries with which we are at war, the War Department is helpless to expedite such reports.

The personal effects of an individual missing overseas are held by his unit for a period of time and are then sent to the Effects Quartermaster, Kansas City, Missouri, for disposition as designated by the soldier.

Permit me to extend to you my heartfelt sympathy during this period of uncertainty.

Sincerely yours,

J. A. ULIO
Major General
The Adjutant General

1 Inclosure
Bulletin of Information

Mac recalled the dropped flyers he'd seen in the towns which had stated clearly, "Any German soldier of any rank who defies the Geneva Convention will be tried in court individually."

Mac's artistic observations of his captors showed him glimpses of their humanity as he tried to hold onto his own. During those long days, weeks and months, Mac's purpose was to capture a likeness of each and every *Fuehrer*, Goon, *Unteroffizier, Grenzpolizei,*

Kommandant and "ferret" he could portray. In the moments when they weren't looking, Mac caught expressions in the stroke of a pencil line on coarse appropriated paper. Drawing from the corner, he encapsulated likenesses in graphite, charcoal and ink, the darkness of a guard's blue eyes narrowed by a contracted heart. He caught in finely-drawn lines, blond hair and azure eyes. Mac saw radiance in a flash of warm memory; a grin emerged from the *unteroffizier's* dark place, illuminating  what could not be spoken. He snagged expressions made solid in lines of what was neither hidden nor lost. By looking closer at a German, Mac saw German men missing their families. His lines took the shape of their yearnings.

Besides Cassie, Neary and Mutt, with whom Mac traded drawings, other Yanks were artists in their own way. Replica German uniforms were sewn from dyed blankets. Pistols and guns were carved from beech bed boards and finished with graphite to look like metal. Escapees wore medallions cast from melted cigarette-pack silver paper. Prisoners "borrowed" a badge from a visiting goon while guards sipped wine and beer, made an impression in a softened soap mold and returned the pin before the loan was noticed. Escapees pulled documents from their pockets, convincingly forged by draftsmen as talented as Mac. Proper stamps printed from a potato or the rubber heel of a boot fooled the guards.

Mac glued a book's pages together and cut a hollow space shaped for a pilfered pair of pliers. Ferrets didn't look inside books. A file bartered from a guard with Red Cross chocolate helped cut a saw out of a scrap of metal.

~

Mac barely had time to dry his shirt when the prisoners were alerted to a possible relocation. Ten thousand men in five compounds awoke in the chilly wind. Drawings were organized, exchanged, and packed in tin boxes. By January 20th, the POWs heard Russian gunfire. By January 25th, the camp's loudspeakers reported that the Russians had advanced through Poland and were 48 miles from Sagan. The Red Cross distributed two D-bars, a quarter pound of cheese, half a pound of oatmeal, half a loaf of bread and sugar, an indication that they would be evacuated soon.

"It's only me..." Dad started a letter to Irene asking for her hand in marriage. He carefully folded his allotted 24 lines of airmail weight paper and addressed it to 421 Central Park, Chicago, Illinois, USA with a licked 40 *pfennig* stamp. In the evacuation, items were destroyed: personal belongings, furniture, inventions, tools, sports equipment, books and old clothes. "The Russians are coming!" reverberated throughout the camp. The men felt the rumblings of tanks in their feet.

The camp was in a frenzy. Inside each reenergized prisoner was disbelief, excitement and fear. Emotions took precious energy. Expectancy was tiring. Reason was submerged below pangs of hunger, survival and covetousness.

From the west, a louder, sustained artillery exploded. Lightning-like explosions appeared at twilight. Large machines rumbled over the vibrating ground. Windows rattled.

Thousands of feet above, aerial duels filled the skies. The *kriegies* lined stones into large "POW" signs to be seen by the pilots. The camp continued operating during the chaos; the prisoners were still under guard. The next morning, Mac listed his effects: two short pencils, three scraps of paper, four sticks of charcoal, a short wire, a role of string, seven rubber-bands, a blanket, coat, pants, three socks, a shirt, a flat-edged razor for shaving and a bar of soap, four packs of cigarettes, a toothbrush and comb, drawings of goons. Russian tanks could be heard in the distance, followed by gunfire.

The Red Cross arrived in a caravan of white trucks. The prisoners received parcels from the neutral country of Switzerland. Mac tallied his own parcel in his head: 8 oz. raisins, 10 oz. salmon, 4 oz. cheese, 2 oz. tinned milk, 15 oz. marmalade, 5 oz. of sardines, 6 oz. prunes, 1 oz. each salt/pepper, 6 oz. chocolate, tea, 6 oz. sugar, 20 oz. biscuits, 20 oz. butter, 13 oz. spam, bread, Klim (milk spelled backwards), cigarettes, soap... And a big chocolate D-bar bar, bitter chocolate with nuts. *Moses can talk about manna all he wants. He's never tasted anything like a D-bar.*

Prisoners prepared for the impending march to an unknown destination. Mac folded his silk map—which had been returned to him—and slipped it up his sleeve with Irene's photo. Mac counted up what he could pack for the march. Everything would be useful—a wire to lace shoes, paper to weave a pad to insulate a jacket. Cups were fabricated from empty coffee cans. Scrap metal utensils were squirreled into jacket pockets. Mac slept on these items and inventoried them each morning. He held back cigarettes, pepper, biscuits and soap to trade.

On January 27th, Berlin sent notice that the prisoners were to be evacuated immediately. The goons announced that the prisoners had thirty minutes to pack their things.

"Hey, you got a smoke?" Barney asked Mac. He had been in sick bay. Mac was relieved Barney would be making the long march. Mac was getting dressed. His thinning hair filled the teeth of his new comb.

"It must be the soap," he joked to Barney to hide his dismay.

Barney slowly got to his feet and dressed for the march. "Guess we're leaving."

South Compound *kriegies* left at 11:00 p.m. and Mac's West Compound followed at 1:00 a.m. on January 28th. It took eight hours to evacuate the entire camp. Flanking guards had counted ten thousand men who filed out of Stalag III. As they left the gate, the West compound sang:

> "I've got sixpence, jolly sixpence
> I've got sixpence to last me all my life.
> I've got sixpence to LEND
> And sixpence to SPEND
> And sixpence to send home to my wife,
> POOR WIFE!"

~

Mac and his fellow *kriegies* were marched south then west out the gates of the gray camp into two feet of snow followed by dogs and a horse-drawn cart of brown bread. *Be careful what you wish for, it could get worse.* A grim trip lay ahead. Every thirty minutes, the column stopped to adjust bedrolls and packs. In a few hours, half-loaves of bread were issued to ease the gasping horses' load. Mac kept the Red Cross jelly, biscuit mix and cigarettes on top of his pack. He traded these with the *volks* along the way for eggs, vegetables and bread.

Mac marched a fifteen-hour day and tasted the freshest provisions he'd eaten since becoming a prisoner. Villagers eagerly traded fresh jam and bread for cigarettes. In the night, they trudged through Hermsdorf and the tiny village os Halbau. Mac perceived the heavy want and sorrow that rushed over the outside world like a deluge. The narrow road wound through Barau, Friewaldau and turned west to the larger town of Priebus. His exchanges with refugees on the road offered a connection with people other than prisoners. *Was it a connection to life, to hope?* He liked them. They were hungry, too. *This is the best food I've had since I landed in Germany.* His woolen sock was his main concern. It kept embedding in a numb blister at the back of his heel. The sock ripped open scabs each night. *Tomorrow I'll try a piece of cotton undershirt between the sock and the foot.*

~

Decades later, Dad handed me one of the books he thought could express to me what he could not about the war, *Monuments Men.* The true story was about an unlikely arrangement of untrained intellects, in fatigues, who banded together to uncover a treasure trove of European art. Two-thousand-feet deep, in a huge underground cavern, after a long descent in an ancient elevator held by ravaged cables, General Eisenhower arrived to inspect the incredible cache. Allies claimed 4,500 gold bars, each weighing twenty-five-pounds, worth about $57,600,000. Millions more, in currency, were confiscated. Priceless paintings were unwrapped. Countless gold and silver fillings, eyeglasses and pocket watches had been stockpiled. This confiscation of the wealth of Germany crippled its military budget.

Dad's thoughts returned to the march out of the prison camp.

"Germans were the first to sign the Geneva Convention articles stating that any officer who attempted to escape was to be treated fairly," he said. "Officers were, I suppose, the privileged, if you could call it privilege. They were under the *Luftwaffe* and generally, outside the orbit of the *Gestapo.* Rumors traveled of shots in the back, POW cremations, tommy-gun beatings and concentration camps."

Dad handed me his purple-and-green German landscape and

explained how Germany looked as he parachuted into Pirmasens. I read my notes about his POW experience to Dad while he was recovering in an intensive care unit. I discovered that one of our favorite television shows, *Hogan's Heroes,* was about Robert Hogan, a B-24 pilot shot down in January of 1945 over Yugoslavia and held in a camp adjacent to Stalag Luft III, where Dad was probably stationed. Bob Crane's television series was about Stalag XIIIC (near Hammelburg).

In third grade, when Dad once tried to show me his scrapbook, I had asked him if being a POW was anything like *Hogan's Heroes.* He simply said,

"Kind of like that. We made ice cream by pouring sugar on the snow."

He closed the book and stopped telling his story. There was little similarity between my father's real-life experience and the *Hogan's Heroes* show, except three significant things: 1) The *Kommandant* did wear a monocle like Colonel Klink; 2) There was a big, fat, goofy sergeant like Sergeant Schulz; and 3) The prisoners had a "secret" radio that gave more accurate information than the German propaganda stations. The colonel allowed BBC and Australian stations to be broadcast. The colonel believed he was serving his Fatherland—not Hitler's causes. Another grim similarity was that both POWs and guards alike were starving to death with only one bowl of cabbage soup and one loaf of black bread per barracks, baked with sawdust filler, daily.

~

1945 January, Surrealism

Mac's first leg of marching in frigid cold weather allowed little rest because the intense cold froze their sweat to chilling ice. A long rest would freeze his trousers to the icy ground. South Compound men, a mile-long column, had trampled the snow ahead of West

Compound. *We'll cross that bridge when we get to it. Don't project.* Mac's replacement boot didn't fit well; after 15 hours of trudging, it pinched his toes and painful sores blistered. *Might get fatally infected.* The boot opened the blistering wounds every morning and they bled all day. *Thank God I packed soap.* Frostbite threatened. Frozen bread couldn't be eaten.

Camp de Prisonniers de guerre

Stalag __XIII D__   Date __30 JAN 1945__

(Seulement No. du Camp, selon les instructions du Commandant)

Je suis prisonnier de guerre en Allemagne et en bonne santé — ~~(ou) légèrement blessé.~~

Nous serons transportés d'ici dans un autre camp au bout de quelques jours. N'écrivez jusqu'à ce que je vous donnerai la nouvelle adresse.

Meilleurs souvenirs

Prénom et nom de famille: __WILLIAM F. McMAHON__

Rang: __2nd LT.   O-2065589__

Détachement: __U.S.A.A.F.__

(Aucun autre détail. — Ecriture lisible.)

77

Mac hadn't received a response from Irene. *Had she received my marriage proposal? Had Irene's response gotten mailed to Stalag III? Would she agree? Would my letter be lost from one camp to the other? Would it be taken by someone? What made me think I should write a marriage proposal? I wish I'd never sent it.* Mac carried her sole telegram to him in his left sleeve. Drawings were in his right sleeve with his silk map.

The men marched further and further toward an unknown camp, hoping it was better that the last. The line stretched out like an accordion. Items that became too heavy to carry were discarded along the littered trail. Men marched in small groups at a leisurely rate, trading along the way. Mac shivered in the biting cold. Half-issues of food portions that barely provided sustenance for the *kriegies*—and the elderly guards—ran low. One meal of barley soup each day was inadequate. Trading cigarettes for eggs was Mac's lifesaver. Snow was their water source.

Just being outside of the fence was tougher. Ghostly shadows of German refugees joined Mac's evacuation march. They arrived in Sternberg in brutal cold, then boarded a cramped boxcar train to Nuremberg that was even more difficult and colder than the march. Their day-long train ride made it through Dresden just a couple weeks before the city was bombed. A hidden radio gave them hope the Allied forces were closing in.

Mac's train stopped near the Nuremberg station.

"Fertig machen!" (Get Ready!) guards ordered, counted, corralled and urged on tired, starving *kriegies*. *Kriegies* carried the elder guards' loads who said *"Muede, muede!"* (Tired!)

Mac's group eventually stopped at a new camp. Every morning, he heard, *"Raus! Raus! Appell! Appell!"* German *unteroffiziers* belted commands. Officers filed from filthy barracks and lined up hundreds of prisoners in rows ten-by-ten on an exercise area of the compound surrounded by frozen mud. The German *obergefreiter* went down the rank and counted: *eins, zwei, drei,* and so forth… One morning, an officer announced:

"I think we have a bad boy here."

The senior officer checked the number against the German

guard's, and the count began again. Sometimes, the POWs would not come to order quickly and that was when an escape had taken place. Prisoners wanted to delay the guards to give the escapee a head start. Mac was never sure what happened to any of them. He wasn't sure what happened to Barney, either. *Maybe he escaped along the road?*

"*Eins, zwei, drei…*" The POWs had disrupted the count, so it began again. They stomped in cesspools, in place, in their own morning-puffed fog. Prisoners had leg cramps but had to keep exercising. The hypnosis of endless rhythms deadened their pain in that monstrous rite… *einhundert, einhundert eins, einhundret zwei…* They stripped wood from the latrines to burn for warmth. Mac rose before dawn for the latrine line. The place was a pig sty. The latrines overflowed in the rain. Mac ate slop, heated in big vats, outside his barracks. Everything they had needed washing. Mac could smell the men who never washed clothes. Those men were covered with vermin bites. Mac slept outside when he could.

There wasn't enough soap to keep clean—not the clothes, not the barracks, not the POWs. Men were covered with skin diseases; scabies resulted from relentless mite bites. Nights were spent pinching lice from clothing. The bartering of soap, razors and food filled their days and nights. It was every man for himself. POWs traded watches and wedding bands for food.

Mac had neither. However, he did have a silk map and his drawings. Mac's mood improved when his map revealed how close the Allied soldiers were. The constantly monitored radios shared daily changing information. Friendly fighter planes flew over the camp regularly. Mac could hear Allied tanks coming across the field. The goons left the watch towers. A jet plane thundered overhead and shook the entire camp. Mac dove into a muddy trench.

~

Mac's group was on the march again. The Germans knew they had lost the war. The landscape was blasted constantly. Mac jumped into ditches when the Army Air Corps and German fighters swooped over and sprayed fire. From behind, friendly fire bullets rained down alongside the gray-faced marchers from fighter planes that splashed Mac with slimy mud. Still, the friendly fire was a reminder that the war's end was near.

Kriegies escaped. Goons helped *kriegies,* hoping for favors later. Icy rains turned the rotting earth into slime; it decomposed Mac's socks into slippery webs that pulled the pickled flesh from his feet. His ears rang from the gun blasts. Abandoned trucks took some of the strafing, and horses and wagons pulled food and gear. Hundreds of refugees from Russian occupation passed through the camp.

Through the cold rainy mist, Mac saw a boy in ragged clothes crawl into a garden for a left-over potato or perhaps a spring garlic. Just under the fence, the boy collapsed and died. A hungry German soldier caught a feral cat by the tail and slammed its head against a tree trunk with a loud *meaaw*.

The guards shouted. Someone had run. Guns fired. Mac watched and waited. Mac marched with the guards he knew. Both German guards and American prisoners knew it was still every man for himself. The guards hoped to become an American—rather than a Russian—prisoner.

The majority of Mac's fellow prisoners were skin and bones. Men collapsed. Some, merely missing. *Maybe escaped? Maybe shot?* His group settled onto a damp pile of hay beside a barn for the night.

~

Mac felt his inner sleeve for his compass, a telegram from Irene. "I'll see you in my dreams," it read. *Keep your wits about you.* Mac looked at the sky for his location in the universe and inward for his heart's guiding purpose. Stars were his pilots in space and time. Star patterns let him know he was headed southeast.

Mac cleaned his raw foot in a small pond. They had yet to learn that Allied Forces had crossed the Rhine, that Patton's Third Army was surging towards them. They trailed onward. POW intelligence passed along the intended policy for the POWs: death by exhaustion. Camp prisoners were to be marched far from invading Russian troops. Starvation and exhaustion tactics would eliminate war crime testimonies from former prisoners if there was ever a war crimes investigation.

April 1945 Wehrmacht Camp VIIA

Mac's group was marched to Moosburg, close to the gas chambers at Dachau. The Werhmacht VIIA camp held over 120,000 international POWs in a facility originally made to hold only a few thousand. Colonel Paul R. "Pop" Goode of Oregon ordered Saturday morning inspections. The men shared dull razors. With the impossible task of trying to keep clean amidst overcrowding and dysentery, the prisoners could only attempt bathing. Other prisoners trimmed their hair when they could. Mac allowed the heavy spring rain to be his shower, in a floor of mud, rather than suffer from fighting over one pump for a hundred men. One spigot offered drinking water.

The overcrowding in the barracks was so severe some men slept on the floor. Walking through the barracks was treacherous. Vermin scurried about.

Mac focused to conserve his strength. Patton's Third Army continued their drive as Allied aircraft whizzed over the camp, some doing barrel rolls. The guards' anxiety skyrocketed; some became friendlier, hoping for American supporters. Mac was one of 120,000 prisoners in the camp. One of 14,891 Americans. One of 300 Chicagoans. He kept to himself. Allied tanks skirmished to the west. Russian tanks resounded from the east. They sang to keep calm, to the tune of "The Battle Hymn of the Republic":

We're a bunch of Yankee soldiers, living deep in Germany.
We're eating soup and black bread, and a beverage they call tea…
Come and get us Georgie Patton, so, we can come rambling home.

April 29, 1945, the camp was liberated. Within hours, the hated *swastika* flag was torn from the city and camp flagpole and Old Glory was hoisted in its place. Grown men cried. Two days later, Mac watched General S. George Patton, with his ivory handled pistol, his polished riding boots, his shiny helmet and full-dress uniform, ride on a Jeep into VIIA. *Seemed like he should be riding a bronze horse.*

© by H. E. Kioux

Prisoners froze. They did not know he was coming and looked more like a bunch of surprised hobos. They cheered at the sight of him. Liberation by the 14th Armored Division was an event anyone there would never forget. Complete chaos ensued with thousands of men crying, praying, laughing, hugging and dancing. They were overcome with great emotion. The camp was surrendered by Major Simoleit, Adjutant at *Stalag Luft III*, who had accompanied the men to VIIA. He and the few remaining guards were driven out of the gate.

~

American Army troops and Red Cross nurses entered the camp. Donuts and coffee were offered. Speakers were put up and American music played, including "Don't Fence Me In" and "At Last." Later, field kitchens fed the men all the food they had missed so much. Stomachs had shrunk, but many men overindulged and threw the food back up. They did not care.

Within a week, Mac and his fellow liberated men were trucked to the local German airfield and flown to Camp Lucky Strike in LeHavre, France to be processed for home. They received back pay, new uniforms, showers, food and slept on cots in big tents.

~

PARIS EDITION

EXTRA THE STARS AND STRIPES EXTRA

Daily Newspaper of U.S. Armed Forces · in the European Theater of Operations

Vol. 1—No. 285   1 Fr.   1 Fr.   Tuesday, May 8, 194

VICTORY

Nazis Reveal Surrender To Western Allies, Russia

Germany announced yesterday that it had surrendered unconditionally to the Western Allies and to Soviet Russia.

There was no official announcement of the surrender from the Allied governments or from Supreme Headquarters of the Allied or Russian Armies, but the British Ministry of Information issued a statement last night declaring that today would be treated as "Victory in Europe Day" in Britain.

Prime Minister Churchill will make "an official announcement at 3 PM today," the ministry said. Simultaneous announcements in Washington and Moscow and at Supreme Headquarters are expected.

In Washington, President Truman said he had agreed with the governments in London and Moscow to make no announcement on the surrender "until simultaneous announcement could be made by the three governments."

Nazis Still Fight Reds At Prague

Russian and U.S. Third Army troops, despite Germany's reported unconditional surrender, continued their sweep into Czechoslovakia yesterday after the Nazi commander there announced his forces still were at war with Russia.

Gen. Patton's famous Fourth Armored Div. last night was reported speeding toward Prague, where partisans and Germans were locked in a struggle for control of the capital. A Czech radio broadcast said Gen. Patton's troops were only 18 miles away and London reports said it was "entirely possible" that American vanguards already were in the city.

Konev Army in Bohemia

Enemy sources said Marshal Ivan Konev's First Ukrainian Army had entered Bohemia from Saxony at a point probably 60 to 55 miles north of Prague.

All fighting stopped yesterday in Breslau, the Silesian capital which has been a battleground since Feb. 17. Marshal Stalin in an order of

(Continued on Page 2)

Prayer, Tears, Laughter —The World Celebrates

People in Allied cities throughout the world yesterday accepted the news of the reported unconditional surrender of Germany as true—despite lack of official announcements from the governments of the U.S., Britain and Russia—and celebrated with prayer, liquor, tears and laughter.

Crowds milled in the streets of the world's great cities—in Times Square, New York; Trafalgar Square and Piccadilly Circus in London, and along the Champs-Elysees, Paris—but it was not a wild jubilee. The absence of a clear-cut official announcement and the piece-by-piece collapse of the German Armies tended to dull the feeling of triumph.

Then, too, the huge casualty lists, the vast war against Japan that still lay ahead, the levelled cities and the shell-pitted fields and the absence of sons, fathers and brothers from homes, checked unrestrained exuberance.

Ticker Tape Showers Wall Street

Ticker tape poured from the office windows of Wall Street and shreds of telephone books from the windows of the Garment Center buildings in the Thirties, and men and women flooded Times Square, waving their arms and trying to express in words their happiness. Liquor flowed inside bars, while people held newspaper extras and devoured the news.

But there was no special need for strict police measures, because the celebrating was orderly. Aristocratic Fifth Avenue in New York City also was covered with ripped sheets of paper which became shapeless messes in the wet streets, but stores remained open and some people seemed more dazed than jubilant there.

On one section of Fifth Avenue, an impromptu conga line was formed, and on another, a group of girls marched spontane-

(Continued on Page 8)

At 9:30 last night King George VI of England sent Gen. Eisenhower a message congratulating him and his armies on the "complete and crushing victory" in Europe.

Despite the apparent surrender by the German high command, hostilities were still in progress in Czechoslovakia, where both American and Russian troops were converging on Prague. Patriots were battling German troops for control of the Czech capital.

The Associated Press broke the news in a story from Rheims, France, that the Allies had officially announced that Germany had surrendered at 0241 hours yesterday morning. It said the surrender took place in the little red school house which is Gen. Eisenhower's headquarters.

Col. Gen. Gustaf Jodl, German army chief of staff, signed for Germany, it was reported.

The German announcement came from Count Schwerin von Krosigk, the new German foreign minister, over the

(Continued on Page 8).

85

Eventually, the men were taken to the harbor by trucks and put onto their ships to make the journey home, traveling in convoys for safety. U-boats still lurked in the Atlantic, so the ships had to zig-zag just to be safe. The weather was stormy and many of the men got seasick.

Mac entered New York and was surrounded by men who cried when they saw the Statue of Liberty. When he disembarked, American flags flew and bands played. The ordeal was over, they were home.

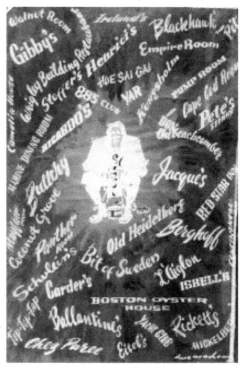

~

Dad and I stared into empty space. *How could I possibly capture all that he knew?* No wonder my dad had not told us anything all those years. While preparing their children for survival, my parents had protected us from knowing the terror Dad had experienced.

I now understand how the $100 bills my Dad had given my mother at Christmas were from skills he'd learned in prison camp. One year, a stack of bills was inside a hollowed-out hardcover book with the pages glued together. That was how prisoners hid stolen tools. "Ferrets" didn't look through the books on the shelf. Another Christmas, the bills were placed in a helium balloon and we kids popped one hundred helium balloons with a hat pin to rain down bills. All the kids scrambled to gather them for Mom. That was like

Uncle Wigglewings dropping parachuting candy for the children in East Berlin that Dad heard about. At Thanksgiving, the family carved Christmas cards out of potato halves to stamp trees and stars, bows and reindeer on folded card stock; this technique was used by prisoners to reproduce and stamp papers to escape from prison.

As Dad came to enjoy the writing of his story, we collaborated even more. He remembered more details, and I jotted down notes. My children grew more curious about their grandfather's experiences

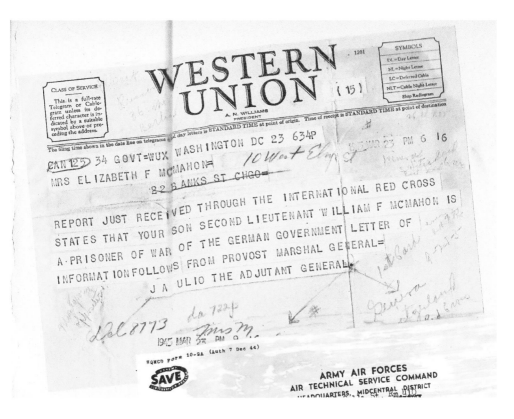

and interviewed him for school PowerPoints and documentaries. The more we all worked together, the broader, the deeper, the more alive Dad's stories became.

Dad had seen incredible poverty and the habits of desperate Germans. He had seen duplicity and simplicity. He had witnessed the comic and the tragic. Above it all, he had seen a really big monstrous thing nearly succeed. He had been part of a dystopian industrial war and part of a better new beginning. Dad had found his purpose and honed his drawing skills.

He was terribly thin by then, with an intense wide-eyed wonder. The only clue to what he'd experienced was a stiff way of turning his left shoulder and a new silent and grave intensity in his smile. He was quiet, stronger in character, yet leery of noises and unexpected cars' backfire. Fireworks were out of the question. It would be months, maybe years, before he unwound enough to allow the interrupted sleep to leave his life.

"No complaints," he told me. "I came out unscathed."

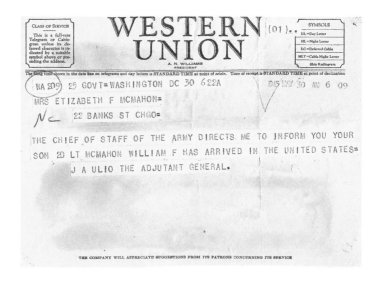

HOMECOMING

Mac returned to an America that had out-fought and out-produced every other country. American soldiers made an incalculable contribution towards ending the war overseas, and the rest of America did what it could back home. When the U.S. needed a workforce, women responded. When the men returned home, the women returned to running households. It was a "can-do" country, and Mac and Irene reunited as changed twenty-five year-olds.

~

Mac greeted Irene with a handshake. No one asked about his life as a camp survivor. Sometimes, he was asked how many enemy soldiers he'd killed. Advertisers glorified the war and equated the win with buying and selling, not killing and dying. Mac learned to shrug,

to put the war out of his mind. He drew and painted to escape again. The GI bill helped him transfer his purpose to an education and a few vittles and vice in their new Near North neighborhood.

He landed safely on Elm Street, in an exuberant Chicago that hosted a beehive of thousands of GIs traveling home by train, plane and boat. Mac was eager to make a long-term commitment to his city and his hometown dove, Irene. Ex-soldiers flooded into a vibrant Chicago, far from their farms, with veterans regarding this wealthy industrial city as the most hospitable in the country. After having seen European cities, flown or sailed across the world, veterans chose the big city to test their new skills. Apartments and houses filled to near bursting as men explored Chicago's music, restaurants and schools to prepare for new jobs. The celebratory openness of the Midwest absorbed thousands of students eager to create a new world.

Irene was still flying the country as a United stewardess, nursing soldiers who were limping home with lightly packed duffels of souvenirs. She saw the broken spirits, the missing arms and bandaged heads of her wounded generation. Irene's sisterhood of Teacher's College forged a camaraderie with art teachers with a social justice message. Irene wanted to be part of traversing the country with Chicago as the main hub.

The first generation of teenagers was born being valued for earning paychecks in the war effort. Irene lifted Mac's spirits. Her voice calmed his unease like a cooing dove. She had sent a telegram response accepting his marriage proposal, but it was never found. They'd returned to each other nonetheless. Each had yearned to be together, yet it would take time for their new selves to meld.

Irene, having built two careers of her own, saw only the best in people. From the first "teenager generation" that worked during high school with extra cash for shopping and cars, Irene added after-church meetings with Saul Alinsky's Catholic Workers, where she honed her natural organizing skills. She emulated the peaceful Dorothy Day as best she could. Congress had cut the education budget and boosted funds for the war effort. The entire world had been at war and she wanted to be a part of it. Certified teachers were sent up to nurse, feed, and care for air passengers and mobilized military with unreliable oxygen and bumpy flights. As United stewardesses, they had migraine headaches, dizziness and nausea, but persevered. Once trained, the criteria for keeping their jobs was to stay unmarried. With Mac back home, he and Irene got engaged.

After a bacon, lettuce and tomato lunch on Michigan Avenue, Mac and Irene walked to the Chicago River to watch the glistening gray-blue water flow past. The tour guide announced facts about the Wrigley building as the boat rippled a path beneath them. They were too polite with each other, too thoughtful. Mac postured self-assurance but appeared tense. Irene treaded lightly. They pretended nothing like a world war had come between them. Conversations flowed about their upcoming wedding, their reception at the

Knickerbocker, flower colors, tablecloths, how many children they would have. *How will our shared passion for travel fit with family? Will we live in Chicago?*

Mac and Irene agreed that travel was their priority. *Maybe a house in the suburbs?* The artists were all moving to the northern suburbs. Mac and Irene's smiles were too intense. Their jokes were strained. They held hands too tightly and hugged liked they never wanted to let go. They had both dared to fly in the newest aircraft technology. They learned to walk together again, understanding they had a shared dream no one else would know. They flowed like water through the dark.

Mac and Irene seemed to be the happiest couple in the world. They rekindled their long-imagined love, at Chez Paree and Chez Paul, Armandos, the Erie Cafe, and Riccardo's. Free at last to be together, they reminisced about high school friends and discussed work. They planned their honeymoon and tried to free their captive selves. Irene wooed Mac until he was gathered safely into her arms.

Mac and Irene danced their wedding dance on July 27th, 1945 at Our Lady of Sorrows Basilica. The church ceremoniously gave the couple scapulas with advice to pray to Blessed Mary, *My Mother, my confidence.* Mac dressed in his Army Lieutenant uniform that morning in his accustomed ritual steps, wishing for good luck while

he shaved with a new razor that was so sharp, it nicked his jaw. None of the invited guests could know Mac's kind of satisfaction. He was alive and marrying Irene. This exuberance was a form of greatness in itself. His mother set down his packed leather aviator's bag to pin a carnation to his lapel. He jolted as a camera flashed.

~

When the catch on the garter caused a run, Irene asked her sister Rita and friend, Charlotte, for new stockings. She'd barely had time from her last air flight to pack for the honeymoon. Rita gathered their best sweaters, blouses and skirts. The sisters exchanged clothing which caused them to look more alike. In a hanging bag was her post-wedding dress for the Knickerbocker Hotel reception. Bess' neighbor arranged for the reception room. In another bag she held the borrowed wedding train which would be attached to her dress at the basilica.

Irene had purchased a simple ivory dress. Long sleeved, embroidered and gathered at her thin waist, the skirt gracefully flowed around her tall heels. In the flurry of scurrying into Our Lady of Sorrow's chamber with her hair intact, the headpiece was pinned and a second application of powder was patted on her cheeks and glistening forehead. She paused to catch her breath. Rita poured three vodkas, and they toasted and sipped, laughing nervously.

Entrance music echoed throughout the vaulted ceiling. Not many soldiers had returned. Several of her stewardess friends were flying that weekend. Her uncle-in-law would escort her down a very long and almost empty aisle. An organ began "The Wedding March." Charlotte and Rita stood beside her. Irene was the first to marry. The press arrived with their cameras.

Irene felt the desire, love and envy of those around her. She held herself gracefully with a straight back and head lifted proudly. Though many of her friends had written to several beaus, there had not been many relationships for any of them in years. Chicago was a hub of military men passing through. Women were anxious to get on with life in their waning twenties. They were anxious to know who, and how, boyfriends would return. Mac's cousin was his best man.

Irene winked in the photographs that ran in the *Chicago Tribune, News Sun* and *Daily Herald*. Mac attempted to calm the adrenaline triggered from the camera flashes. He squelched the terror inside. The scapula hung under Mac's shirt; Irene's was in her clutch. Unencumbered by a beau, Mary Marg Wolf was drawn into the Basilica by the music. She peeked in to see their wedding day and imagined her own. She quietly settled into the back pew as Mac and Irene recited their vows, whispered "I do," slipped gold ring bands onto each other's third left finger, and turned to face the praying cluster of hopeful faces.

All were celebrating the end of the war, rations, separation and coming together. Mac and Irene ducked arm-in-arm through the gathered group of family friends on the Basilica steps to whoops, hoots and cascading rice. Irene's parents had been married there in quieter—but just as uncertain—times. Her grandparents on both sides had been married in New Jersey.

Mac gazed into Irene's gray hazy-blue eyes. She had a solemn, warm, girl-like calm face. There was something ethereal about her, as if she always gracefully carried a bouquet of fresh flowers. Irene looked into Mac's sky-blue wide and excited eyes. She handed him her suitcase. He had the keys to Bess' Buick. They were giddy with their plans for a road trip. She watched his agile, delicate hands—artist's hands—take the steering wheel.

They drove to the Knickerbocker with tin cans rattling behind them. Only recently, tin had been rationed. Soap was flagrantly wasted to write *Just Married* on the back window. They passed the sound of waves on the outer drive. Combining food stamps, Mac's GI bill salary, and a reduced-price reception hall, they celebrated a glorious wedding. Photos captured every posed moment of cake-cutting and feeding each other's forkloads of Gram's whipped cream frosted angel food cake, Bess' brown-sugar dipped figs, dark-chocolate macaroons and William's pineapples from California.

Free at last! Together finally! Mac and Irene settled into their suite in the Knickerbocker while the celebration continued below. Calming waves were still breaking along the Streeterville embankment.

In the near future, it would be a quite ordinary thing for young people to do, but for that time, Mac and Irene were celebrating one of Chicago's first postwar weddings.

After postponing Mac's military check-in, they traversed the states by car to honeymoon in Niagara Falls, then north to Alderbrook, New York, where Mac's parents had been married. Their compromise was to honeymoon in the Adirondacks and celebrate with the Franklins and McKillip cousins.

~

As a redefined, eager housewife with a charmed life of marital silver, china and a table of friends, Irene longed for travel.

"When I was flying, I felt I was on the edge of my life. The closest I'd ever felt to being me in the fear of the unknown. I could feel my blood moving under my skin, my fingernails growing. My hair and face were full of electricity! I glowed silver. When I was flying, I was in control of myself. I knew who I was," she'd said to Mac. After marriage, stewardesses weren't allowed to work, to fly, to earn.

Mac and his new bride flew together for the first time to Miami for a week at the Army Air Force Separation Base for Mac's discharge from service. If serving in war wasn't enough, a hurricane blew in after they landed. They were newly married, away from Chicago and

hoping to extend their honeymoon with their first flight. A knock on the door surprised Mac. A frightened, newly married Charlotte and Len Monday, their friends, entered to ride out the storm. That was the way it was.

~

Irene and Mac walked home from Institute of Design lectures along Clark Street in Chicago. Mac knew that art was as old as humans; art says, "*I existed.*" Art always had been, still was and would always will be a necessity of life. At the lecture, they heard that art was an indispensable means of merging the person with the community to create a perpetual equilibrium with everyone's surrounding world. Mac learned the process to seize the moment, transform his impression into memory and express that memory into material form and project onto society from Lazlo Maholy

Nagy. In this process, he took possession of what nature imposed on the social order, worked his magic with pencil and paper and gave a new insight. Irene got it. She, too, saw art's importance to reshaping society.

What Mac later called *the 95% sweat* was to know his trade, enjoy it, understand the rules, skills, forms and conventions and tame the subject into a symphony of lines and color on paper. This process of reasoning purified his creativity. His rhythm of lines delighted his viewers to look into the difficult imagery he had witnessed. Moholy Nagy invented, taught branding and packed a lunch to draw on the street. He taught Mac how to project his work onto society to nudge it in the right direction.

~

At the end of June 1947, Irene and Mac's first child was born, William Franklin McMahon Jr. Mac and Irene McMahon had nine blue-eyed children who taught, wrote and made art while raising families in Europe, Asia, across the United States, and in Chicago. Irene's travel writing was for a weekly column and many newspapers and magazines. She received awards for her writing, including the Mark Twain Award for Travel Writing. Franklin McMahon's art has been collected by the Art Institute of Chicago, Smithsonian, Library of Congress, Princeton University Art Museum and the National Air and Space Museum. His artwork has been published by too many magazines, books and newspapers to list, yet includes *The New York Times, The New Yorker, Chicago Tribune, Look* and *Life*. He was awarded as an Illinois State Treasure, three Emmys® and a Peabody® for films and videos, inducted into the Society of Illustrators Hall of Fame, Martin Luther King Award for Civil Rights Achievement and honorary degrees from Loyola University and Lake Forest College. His films have been broadcast by PBS, WTTW and CBS. *Martin, Douglas (March 7, 2012). "Franklin McMahon, Who Drew the News, Dies at 90". The New York Times*

AAF Silk Map

William Franklin McMahon: Grand Marshall of the Lake Forest Day Parade

Acknowledgments

Mac & Irene owes a great debt to scholars who helped give a context to the WWII story my parents found too hard to tell. Many scholars were introduced during Yale for Life (now Everscholar) that Andrew Lipka orchestrated for Jay Winters to lecture with poetry, film, and literature colleagues who have filled my shelves with worn-out books. A few books are: Eugene Rogan's *The Fall of the Ottomans: the Great War in the Middle East*, Elie Wiesel's *Survival in Auschwitz*, Eugene B. Sledge's *With the Old Breed*, Ernest Hemingway's *A Farewell to Arms*, Michael C C Adams' *The Best War Ever: America and World War II*, Ernst Junger's *Storm of Steel* and Pat Barker's *Regeneration Trilogy. Interrogation to Liberation* by Michael Eberhardt walked me through Stalag IIII and Wermacht VIIA. My sister, Michelle McMahon Kubota, shared sleuthing and research that gave a Chicago historical context. Ragdale Foundation offered residencies that allowed precious focused time for challenging sections and the community to reflect with me to find my voice. It took a nation of many generous listeners and readers at Story Studio, Off Campus Writer's Workshop, Ninety-Days-to-Finish, Chicago Literary Club for deadlines, readings and feedback. Thanks to Nadine Kenney Johnstone, Fred Shafer, Rachael Herron, and the encouragement of my writing group.

Neighbors and friends who read and gave insights: John Coon, Joe Berton, Scott Jacobs, my book group (who may recognize passages from our reading). *Mac & Irene* owes great thanks for the visions of Heather Buchanan, John Knight, Eileen Pollack and Gayle Weinstein.

Thanks to my family: Dan, Brendan, Irene and Aubrey who listened, discussed and encouraged my finding the *Mac & Irene* story that binds us together by knowing our common past. *Mac & Irene* would not exist without each and every one of you.

About the Author

Margot McMahon, daughter of Franklin McMahon, is an internationally-acclaimed artist and sculptor with work exhibited at the Smithsonian and around the world in public and private collections.

Her work appears in the permanent collections of Yale University, the John D. and Catherine T. MacArthur Foundation, the John D. MacArthur State Park, The Museum of Contemporary Art in Chicago, The National Portrait Gallery, the Chicago History Museum, The Chicago Botanic Garden and Soka Gakkai International. Over a period of five years, McMahon explored and interpreted her Irish Catholic heritage in the creation of art for St. Patrick's Church in Lake Forest, Illinois.

Margot earned an MFA from Yale University and taught sculpture and drawing at the School of the Art Institute of Chicago, DePaul University and Yale University. She lives in Chicago with her husband and visiting three grown children.
www.MargotMcMahon.com

https://www.chicagotribune.com/columns/blair-kamin/ct-biz-emmett-till-house-museum-kamin-20200921-wemzzj4xrbgpxl7jalqmpyt4le-story.html

Lightning Source UK Ltd.
Milton Keynes UK
UKHW050231021021
391507UK00005B/144/J

9 781737 987604